# Stern's Guide To

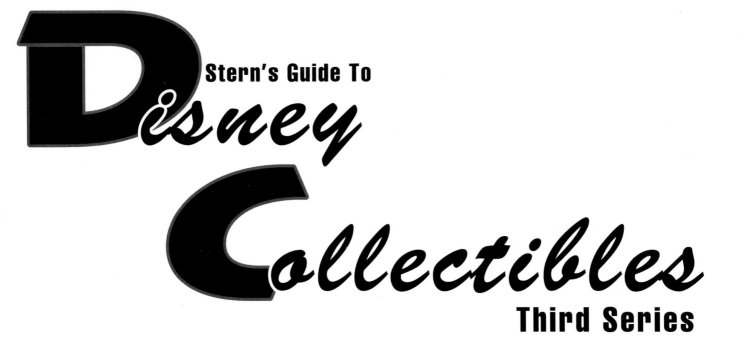

**Disney Collectibles**

**Third Series**

*Michael Stern*

**COLLECTOR BOOKS**

*A Division of Schroeder Publishing Co., Inc.*

The current values in this book should be used only as a guide. They are not intended to set prices, which vary from one section of the country to another. Auction prices as well as dealer prices vary greatly and are affected by condition as well as demand. Neither the Author nor the Publisher assumes responsibility for any losses that might be incurred as a result of consulting this guide.

On the Cover:
Top: DONALD DUCK RUBBER SQUEAK TOY. G – $375.00, Ex/M – $425.00.
Center, left: PINOCCHIO BAYARD FRENCH ALARM CLOCK. G – $350.00, Ex/M – $400.00.
Center right: MICKEY MOUSE NIGHT LIGHT. G – $350.00, Ex/m – $450.00.
Bottom, left: CELLULOID MICKEY MOUSE. G –$3,000.00, Ex/M – $3,500.00.
Bottom, right: FUN-E-FLEX PLUTO THE PUP. G – $200.00, Ex/M – $250.00.

## Searching For A Publisher?

We are always looking for knowledgeable people considered to be experts within their fields. If you feel that there is a real need for a book on your collectible subject and have a large comprehensive collection contact Collector Books.

*Cover design: Beth Summers*
*Book design: Joyce Cherry*

Additional copies of this book may be ordered from:

COLLECTOR BOOKS
P.O. Box 3009
Paducah, Kentucky  42002–3009

$18.95. Add $2.00 for postage and handling.

Copyright: Michael Stern, 1995

Printed by IMAGE GRAPHICS, INC., Paducah, Kentucky

# Contents

# Acknowledgments

To all the great friends that I've made and the people I have met while in pursuit of Disneyana.

To Michelle Farmer for her diligence in putting my notes into book form.

To my family, friends, and business partner who must endure my collecting "craziness."

# Introduction

There's still no greater thrill than to find a Disneyana collectible not previously seen before. Since the last edition was published, the Disneyana marketplace has gone through quite a transformation. The most basic economic principle of supply and demand has encompassed the collectors of Disney memorabilia. The demand for these artifacts of the past has grown dramatically and the supply has just as dramatically decreased. This is not to say that one cannot find Disneyana available; it's just that it's most difficult because the number of collectors has grown.

Lack of supply, and more demand for it, has pushed the prices of high-quality, early Disneyana memorabilia much higher. Who could have fathomed that a black and white cell from "Orphan's Benefit" would have sold for $450,000 or that a Mickey Mouse Cowboy Knickerbocker Doll would fetch $16,000 at auction.

Disneyana is a comic art form, and the appreciation of prices of this art form parallels the increase in the values of all forms of artwork. It could be said that the owning of Disneyana is like owning quality stocks and bonds — an excellent investment that increases in value on a yearly basis. The added value is that whereas stock and bonds are tucked away in a safe or vault; your Disneyana collectibles can be displayed and enjoyed on a daily basis. I call it "double appreciation."

Mickey Mouse and the gang continue to be the most sought after of any characters in the comic collectible field. With the addition of Disney theme parks in Europe and Japan, Disneyana collecting has become international. Each day more and more people join the field of Mickey Mouse fanatics who live and breathe for that new piece to add to their collection. The number of Disneyana collectors is growing and the intensity of these Disney enthusiasts is overwhelming. Many publications and auction catalogs are available for those wishing to acquire Disney memorabilia through the mail.

The following are publications that contain valuable information on a variety of Disneyana topics:

The Inside Collector
225 Main Street, Suite 300
Northport, NY 11708-1737

Antique Toy World
P. O. Box 34590
Chicago, IL 60634

The following are reputable mail and phone bid auction houses that contain Disneyana:

A Mouse in the House
P. O. Box 2183
Clarksville, IN 47129

'Tiques
Highway 34 R 1 Box 49B
Old Bridge, NJ 08857
(908) 679–8212

Smith House Toys
P. O. Box 336
Eliot, ME 03903

Robert Coup
P. O. Box 348
Leola, PA 17603
(717) 656–7780

New England Auction Gallery
P. O. Box 2273
W. Peabody, MA 01960–7273
(503) 535–3140

All of the photographs in this book are taken from my personal collection. I have been collecting for 15 years. It took a lot of leg work, a multitude of patience, and a lot of luck being in the right place at the right time. All of these items have been acquired since the publication of the first two books. Disney collectibles are still out there. They do exist, and though it's not always easy, they can be found by today's collectors.

My hope is that this book will help assist and broaden one's scope so that when acquiring a piece of Disney memorabilia, it can be dated and its price put into perspective.

# Pricing Information

The price guide for Disneyana collectibles is to be used as a point of reference before buying or selling an item. Any price guide tends to be subjective in nature, and I've used the sources available to me to arrive at what I think are accurate price points in today's marketplace. The Disney toy market can change dramatically in a very short span of time.

I have determined the prices for each item based on a number of factors and sources:

    1. What I paid for each item.
    2. Auction catalogs.
    3. Mail auction price realized lists.
    4. Toy and doll show prices.
    5. *Antique Trader* ads.

I feel the prices suggested are excellent estimates of what each item is actually worth. The basic law of economics—supply and demand—can shoot holes through any price guide. The adage that the worth of a toy is what someone will pay for it is still prevalent for today's collectors.

Emotion and the strong desire of wanting to add a certain piece to your collection will result in paying more.

The following descriptions relate to the condition of the toy and how they are priced accordingly.

## GOOD CONDITION

The toy is in working order, has been used, shows general wear and tear. The toy must look fairly clean with little or no rust.

## EXCELLENT, MINT CONDITION

The toy is clean and looks as if it was never used. It is complete and all functions are operative. Mint applies to mint in the box (MIB) and means the toy is in its original packaging. In many cases, the box is worth more than the item itself.

# Pie-eyed
# Mickey and Minnie Mouse

When Mickey Mouse first appeared in the black and white comic film short "Steamboat Willie" in 1928, his creator must have hoped for a cartoon character who would at least survive through several short films. Walt Disney may have realized that he had hit upon something special with the creation of Mickey, but he could not have had an idea of the genuine cultural phenomenon his little rodent would create.

For over 60 years, his squeaky voice, rat-like features, snout nose, and big shoes became bench marks that made him famous. He was not a hero who won out with physical force. Mickey always got to where he was by hard work (and sometimes even pain) combined with a little bit of luck. He came to represent the best in all of us.

Early in his cartoon animation career, Walt Disney learned the importance of his characters having real feelings and emotions which could be displayed on the screen. Without this depth of character, the little fictional beings he created would have been as flat as the celluloid upon which they were penned. Instead of simple cartoon foolery, Disney insisted upon well rounded, interesting, and likable cartoon characters. As a

result, it is Mickey Mouse above all others who stands as the symbol of popular American culture of the 1930's. Even though there was a host of cartoon characters who arrived on the scene in this decade; it was Mickey's appearance in 1928 and his subsequent evolution through the 1930's and 1940's as both a corporate symbol and the subject of American marketing genius that makes him the most interesting of all.

Walt Disney may have begun his animation career as an artist, but he quickly developed a reputation as one who could inspire others with his tremendous imagination and the ability to turn his ideas into actual film possibilities. He was not a merchandiser or a retailer, yet even in his thirties he had the savvy to realize that the popularity of his mouse was worth more than simply movie rentals or theatre admissions.

Enter a man by the name of Kay Kamen, and the rest is merchandising history. Walt had a studio to run with tight production schedules and an ever-increasing staff. Kamen had the time, energy, and most importantly, the business know-how to take a lot of good ideas for potential Mickey Mouse merchandise and turn them into simply fantastic toys! This is not to say Kamen was the toy designer or inventor of the great 1930's Mickey toy—he was the facilitator, the man who put the right toy licensing contracts into the hands of the right toy people. As a result, such big names as Parker Brothers, Whitman Publishing, Louis Marx, Milton-Bradley, Fisher-Price, Ingersol, Lionel, and Ohio Art, among many others, quickly jumped on the Disneyana bandwagon.

Collectors of Disneyana realize they are challenged with many important decisions to make. Collecting Disneyana in general is quite fulfilling for a while, but the sheer amount of merchandise in the marketplace makes it financially impossible to collect everything that is out there. Furthermore, space limitations in the average home usually force even novice collectors to decide upon certain specialty areas within a few years. And if there is one common character that nearly every Disneyana collector holds in common, it is Mickey Mouse. Since the early 1930's, Mickey toys are the virtual flagships of Disneyana collecting, nearly all collectors try to find at least a few rare 1930's Mickey pieces.

The 1930's may be synonymous with the Great Depression in America but it certainly did not adversely affect the appearance of hundreds of wonderful Mickey Mouse toys brought onto the market. Maybe they were purchased as a diversion a way to keep the kids from realizing how bad things really were. After all Mickey Mouse was not geared exclusively to a child audience; adults went nuts over Mickey Mouse too!

Today's collector of 1930's vintage Mickey Mouse memorabilia still faces a wide assortment of interesting toys available. The old folk tale that "the good stuff just isn't out there" is simply untrue. Even though Disneyana in general underwent a price renaissance in the late 1980's, with prices on many items seemingly doubling overnight, a cavalcade of dealers and collectors brought wonderful merchandise out onto the market. The supply is still there, and the demand continues to be great. So be prepared to pay for the rare and quality toys that you desire. It's getting harder and harder to find a Mickey Mouse 1930's toy bargain these days.

Another interesting phenomenon that affects the pricing of vintage Mickey Mouse toys is that Mickey is collectible to others in toy collecting circles. Mickey Mouse is the most recognizable character. Mickey toys are passionately sought out by general toy collectors, comic character toy collectors, animation art enthusiasts, tin windup collectors, and popular art collectors in addition to Disneyana enthusiasts. All of this interest in Mickey toys helps to fuel the fires that keep Disneyana prices generally higher than many other similar vintage toys on the market today.

For the sake of the novice collectors who use this book as a basic introduction to Disneyana collecting, several simple identification notes should be helpful. And for the advanced, experienced collector who doesn't want to review what is already known, just skip to the next paragraph. When dealing with identification of vintage Disneyana, three basic and simple copyright markings can help establish the age and date of a toy. The earliest Mickey Mouse toys are simply marked "Walt E. Disney" or W.D. Disney or W.D.E. Toys with this copyright marking are from the very late 1920's to the early 1930's. The greatest bulk of vintage 1930's Disneyana items are marked "Walt Disney Enterprises" which was the marketing and licensing branch of the Disney Studio from the mid-1930's until the release of *Pinocchio* in 1939. After *Pinocchio* the copyright identification switches to the more familiar "Walt Disney Productions." Therefore, the marking of "Walt Disney Productions" should signal to the collector that a toy is from the 1940's or later.

Many novice collectors will make the statement, "I only collect Disneyana marked 'Enterprises,' " and that is probably not whet they mean to say. Most of these collectors are forgetting that items from the very early 1930's would not be marked "Enterprises" since the term did not come into existence until the marketing/licensing branch was established. Hence, these collectors would probably be more than happy to collect any of the very early items marked simply "Walter E. Disney."

The pictorial section on pie-eyed Mickey opens up with Plate 1 of an extremely rare doll. This doll was designed and produced by Charlotte Clark and is the first doll known to be licensed and approved by Walt Disney. Charlotte Clark and her six helpers produced 300 to 400 dolls per week. This original Charlotte Clark doll is marked on the underside of the doll's foot. It is stamped "Walt Disney's 'Mickey Mouse' Design Patent Applied For." The doll is made of a velveteen material.

The Emerson Mickey Mouse Radio pictured in Plate 2 is rare but the box is extremely hard to find. The radio is made of wood and is an example of an item produced in the 1930's by a company still in existence today.

The Mickey Mouse projector in Plate 3 is the only one I've ever seen. The projector was produced by Safe-Toy Cinema. The graphics on the box are fantastic. The decal on the projector is an

8

excellent example of pie-eyed Mickey.

Plate 4 is an early example of a German ceramic piece. This early condiment set depicts the German 1930's Mickey look. It is marked by a number on the back of the sugar container. These pieces are very desirable and highly sought after by collectors.

The Mickey Mouse radio pictured in Plate 5 is a short wave radio from Australia. This is the only type of short wave radio Disney ever produced. It is made of Bakelite and marked on the front Mickey "Astor" Mouse.

The very rare and very desirable Lionel Mickey Mouse Circus Train is shown in Plates 6 & 7. This toy is on every Disney collector's top ten. Shown here with its original box and composition conductor. The train also came with a series of cardboard punch-outs which could be assembled into a very large and impressive circus tent to stand in the middle of the oval track. A complete version of the Lionel train set is indeed a rarity and commands a very high price.

Plate 8 pictures a Mickey Mouse Flashlight with the original box. The flashlight was produced by the USA Lite Company. The colorful lithography on the flashlight itself is fantastic.

The Mickey Mouse movie projector pictured in Plate 9 was made by the Keystone Company of Boston. The metal projector played 16 millimeter safety films.

The Rocking Horse Mickey wood and celluloid windup pictured in Plate 10 features Mickey astride a wooden horse. This toy probably best depicts the combination of wood and celluloid design found on many of the early 1930's Disney toys.

The Mickey Mouse Pencil Box shown in Plate 11 is quite unique. Made by the Joseph Dixon Crucible Co. this particular pencil box includes the business card of the salesman for the Dixon Company. It also shows the hard to find Dixon map, Mickey Mouse pencils, eraser, and other school implements.

In Plate 12 is a mint example of the Ohio Art Washing Machine. This piece is one of the most graphic tin items. The lithography of Mickey and Minnie doing their wash is beautiful. The box that is also pictured is impossible to find and really enhances the value of the washing machine.

In Plate 13 is is an excellent Mickey example of how a Fun-E-Flex figure was utilized with another object to enhance sales. This Mickey Mouse rowboat complete with oars is marked accordingly on the side.

A 1937 box of Mickey Mouse Cookies shown in Plate 14 verifying once again that anything that could utilize the popularity of Mickey Mouse to sell the product was used. The Walt Disney Enterprises marking was still used in 1937.

In Plate 15 a store display for Walt Disney Character Barettes is shown. Even though marked Walt Disney Productions, this piece shows pie-eyed Mickey and Minnie probably indicating production in 1939 – 1940. Store displays are always hard to find and will brighten up any room.

In Plate 16 a Mickey and Pluto Bisque is shown. This is a rare bisque figure and the only one I know of that uses a string and molds two figures together. The quality of bisque is determined by the amount of paint remaining. This bisque has 100% of its original paint.

The French Cine Mickey Projector in Plate 17 is very simplistic with no graphics but the box is another story. The box is bright and vivid and an excellent example of a foreign item.

In Plate 18 another child's item is shown. The plastic Mickey Mouse Children's Cup was shatterproof, stainproof, non-Corrosive, sanitary, durable and had Mickey Mouse on it. What mother wouldn't buy that for her child?

Some of the hardest items to find are the German tin pieces. Pictured, in Plate 19 is the Mickey Mouse Sparkler produced by the Nifty Toy Company and imported to the United States by Geo. Borgfeldt & Co. Don't be deterred from buying this piece if the sparks don't fly—most don't.

Plate 20 pictures the Mickey Mouse Garden Roller, an English piece that was actually used to work in the garden. This metal contraption makes a great display piece.

Plate 21 shows an example of a ceramic German Mickey Mouse Knife Rest. Note the circular eyes are different from the pie-eyed but common in the German china pieces from the early 1930's.

In Plate 22 Mickey Mouse Pops is pictured. This was an item given as a gift featuring five lollipops. It was manufactured by Brandle & Smith Co. Mickey's eyes and hands move and a poem is included inside with little Mickeys and Minnies surrounding it.

In Plate 23 is pictured a superb example of early Mickey Mouse Dolls. Cowboy Mickey and Cowgirl Minnie were manufactured by the Knickerbocker Toy Company. They realized that you could take the standard Mickey doll and put a costume on it and increase sales dramatically.

The Mickey Mouse Pocket Watch is shown in Plate 24. It was made by the Ingersoll Company and came complete with watch fob. The back of the watch is embossed with a Mickey Mouse image.

Pictured in Plate 25 is the Mickey Mouse Treasure Chest Bank sold in Chicago at the 1933–1934 World's Fair. Pictured on the bank are exhibits at the World's Fair and the saying "Be thrifty — save your coins."

The Mickey Mouse Musician Bisque is pictured in Plate 26. The accordion player is from a set of four and is 5" inches tall. Bisque figurines were hand painted and mass produced in Japan. It is hard to find a bisque figurine with the original tail.

PLATE 1 - *MICKEY MOUSE CLOTH DOLL was designed and manufactured by Charlotte Clark. It was the first licensed Mickey Mouse doll. Note the pie eyes and four fingered hands. It is marked on the foot. G – $2,000.00, Ex/M – $3,000.00.*

PLATE 2- *MICKEY MOUSE RADIO was manufactured by the Emerson Company. It is made of wood. G – $1,700.00, Ex/M – $2,500.00.*

PLATE 3 - *MICKEY MOUSE PROJECTOR was made by Safe-Toy Company. It showed 9.5mm films. This projector was produced in England. G – $800.00, Ex/M – $1,200.00.*

PLATE 4 - *MICKEY MOUSE GLAZED CERAMIC CONDIMENT HOLDER was made in Germany. The number 2820 is inscribed on the back of the piece. G – $1,000.00, Ex/M – $1,200.00.*

PLATE 5 - *MICKEY MOUSE SHORT WAVE RADIO was made in Australia by Astor. This is the only Mickey Mouse radio known to be made of Bakelite. G – $3,000.00, Ex/M – $3,500.00.*

PLATE 6 - *MICKEY MOUSE LIONEL CIRCUS TRAIN and waving composition barker figure is one of the top ten wanted Disney toys. G – $8,000.00, Ex/M – $12,500.00.*

PLATE 7 - MICKEY MOUSE LIONEL CIRCUS TRAIN BOX shows great graphics. The cars are early examples of beautiful tin lithography. G – $8,000.00, Ex/M – $12,500.00.

PLATE 8 - MICKEY MOUSE FLASHLIGHT was made by the USA Lite Company. There are camping scenes on the flashlight. It is marked W.D. Enterprises. G – $1,000.00, Ex/M – $1,200.00.

PLATE 9 - *MICKEY MOUSE MOVIE PROJECTOR was manufactured by the Keystone Company. The protector showed safety films. G – $600.00, Ex/M – $650.00.*

PLATE 10 - *CELLULOID MICKEY MOUSE is found on a wooden horse. There is a wind-up mechanism on the side of the horse. A very early example of a motion toy. G – $3,000.00, Ex/M – $3,500.00.*

**PLATE 11** - *MICKEY MOUSE PENCIL BOX made by the Dixon Crucible Company. This box is complete with Mickey Mouse pencil and eraser and rare Dixon map. It is marked Walt Disney. G – $200.00, Ex/M – $225.00.*

**PLATE 12** - *MICKEY MOUSE WASHING MACHINE was made by Ohio Art Company. This is an excellent example of tin lithography. The box is almost impossible to find. G – $1,700.00, Ex/M – $2,000.00.*

PLATE 13 - *MICKEY MOUSE WOODEN ROWBOAT utilizes Fun-E-Flex Mickey Mouse. The boat is marked Mickey Mouse 28. G – $2,300.00, Ex/M – $2,700.00 set.*

PLATE 14 - *MICKEY MOUSE COOKIES were made by the National Biscuit Company. They were made with Arrowroot flour. The box is marked 1937, Walt Disney Enterprises. G – $300.00, Ex/M – $350.00.*

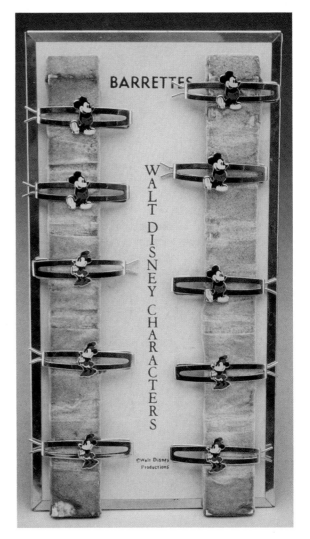

PLATE 15 - MICKEY MOUSE CHARACTER BARRETTES are on an original store display. The barrettes are made of metal. G – $800.00, Ex/M – $850.00.

PLATE 16 - MICKEY MOUSE & PLUTO BISQUE is one of the rarer bisque figurines. It is the only one that has two Disney characters molded together. Mickey's left arm is movable. It was made in Japan. The paper label on the bottom of the foot reads "Mickey Mouse Copr. 1920 1930 by Walter E. Disney." G – $750.00, Ex/M – $1,000.00.

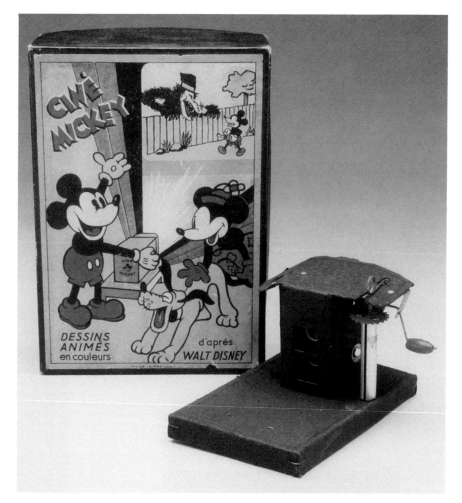

PLATE 17 - *MICKEY MOUSE PRO-JECTOR is a rare French piece. The graphics on the box are superb. The projector itself is very simplistic. G – $800.00, Ex/M – $900.00.*

PLATE 18 - *MICKEY MOUSE CHILD'S CUP is made of plastic and is shatterproof, stainproof, non-corrosive, sanitary, and durable. G – $550.00, Ex/M – $600.00.*

PLATE 19 - MICKEY MOUSE SPARKLER *was made by the Nifty Toy Company and imported by the Geo. Borgfeldt & Co. The sparkler is tin. G – $2,000.00, Ex/M – $2,200.00.*

PLATE 20 - MICKEY MOUSE GARDEN ROLLER *is made of metal and is English. G – $400.00, Ex/M – $425.00.*

PLATE 21 - *MICKEY AND MINNIE KNIFE REST is ceramic and an example of an early German piece. G – $150.00, Ex/M – $175.00.*

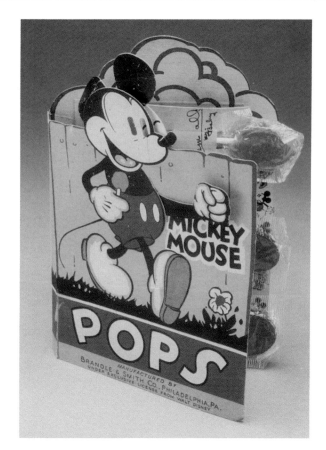

PLATE 22 - *MICKEY MOUSE POPS was made by Brandle & Smith Co. and was given as a gift during the 1930's. It came complete with 5 lollipops. G – $500.00, Ex/M – $600.00.*

PLATE 23 - *COWBOY MICKEY AND COWGIRL MINNIE DOLLS were made by the Knickerbocker Toy Company. The shoes are composition. Minnie's outfit is made of leather. G – $2,200.00, Ex/M – $2,500.00 set.*

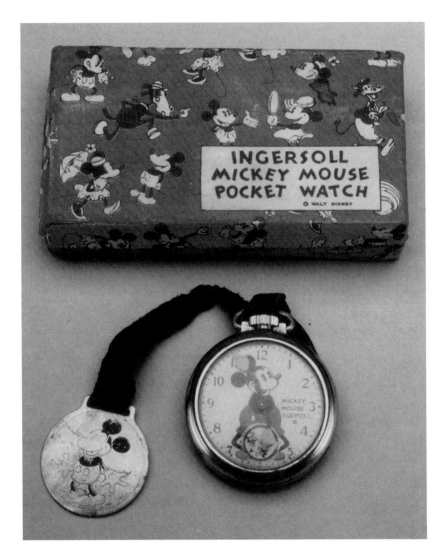

**PLATE 24** - *MICKEY MOUSE POCK-ET WATCH was made by Ingersoll and comes with Mickey watch fob. It utilizes a revolving Mickey second dial. G – $700.00, Ex/M – $850.00.*

**PLATE 25** - *MICKEY MOUSE WORLD'S FAIR BANK was sold at the Chicago's World's Fair in 1933–1934. "Be Thrifty —save your coins." G – $600.00, Ex/M – $625.00.*

**PLATE 26 - *MICKEY MOUSE ACCORDION PLAYER BISQUE FIGURE is 5½"
tall. This musical fellow is one of an entire set of musical Mickeys. G –
$500.00, Ex/M – $550.00.***

**PLATE 27** - *MICKEY MOUSE TOP made by the Fritz Bueschel Company in the 1930's. This is the harder to find orange color. G – $250.00, Ex/M – $300.00.*

**PLATE 28** - *MICKEY MOUSE ASHTRAY is made of a gauze-like material. It is marked on the bottom "by consent Walt Disney, made in England." G – $500.00, Ex/M – $525.00.*

PLATE 29 - *MICKEY MOUSE NIGHT LIGHT was made by the MicroLite Company. This "Kiddy Lite" is battery operated. G – $350.00, Ex/M – $450.00.*

PLATE 30 - *MICKEY MOUSE DOLL was produced by Dean's Rag and is English. The eyes are beads. Note the markings on Mickey's neck. G – $500.00, Ex/M – $525.00.*

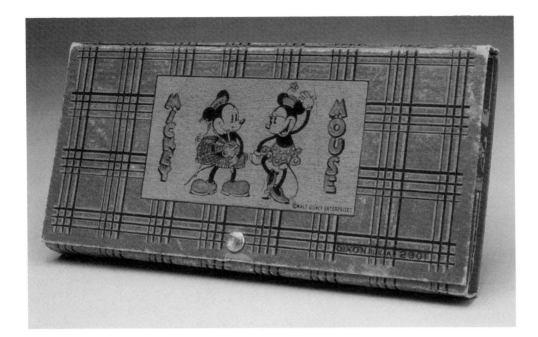

PLATE 31 - *MICKEY MOUSE DIXON PENCIL BOX is marked Walt Disney Enterprises. G – $100.00, Ex/M – $125.00.*

PLATE 32 - *MICKEY MOUSE PAAS EASTER PARADE STORE DISPLAY is for Transfer-o-s which children used to decorate their Easter eggs. They were made from pure food colors. G – $350.00, Ex/M – $400.00.*

PLATE 33 - *MICKEY MOUSE CARD HOLDER is made of celluloid. G – $225.00, Ex/M – $250.00.*

PLATE 34 - *MICKEY MOUSE SONGBOOK BISQUE is a hard one to find. Each bisque was hand painted in Japan. The paper label on the foot reads "Mickey Mouse, DES.PAT 82802, by Walter E. Disney." G – $400.00, Ex/M – $425.00.*

**PLATE 35** - *MINNIE MOUSE WOODEN FIGURES are Fun-E-Flexs. The original dresses really enhance the value of these figures. Very important is the amount of the label that is still present. G – $300.00, Ex/M – $325.00.*

PLATE 36 - MICKEY MOUSE FUN-E-FLEX WOODEN FIGURES *are shown. Beware of replaced ears on these figures. G – $300.00, Ex/M – $325.00.*

PLATE 37 - MICKEY MOUSE ASHTRAY *was made in Bavaria and is very sought after. G – $100.00, Ex/M – $125.00.*

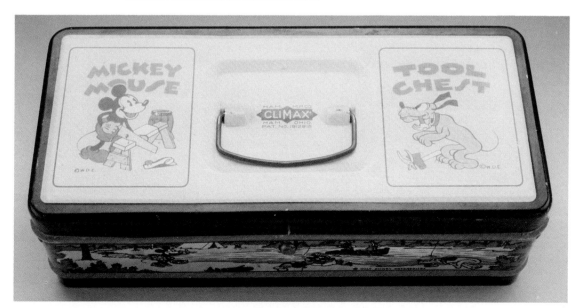

PLATE 38 - MICKEY MOUSE TOOL CHEST, 1936 manufactured by the Hamilton Metal Products Company. This box features full-color tin lithography on all sides and is marked "Walt Disney Enterprises." G – $350.00, Ex/M – $400.00.

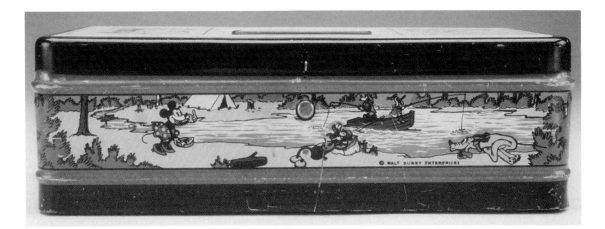

PLATE 39 - *MICKEY MOUSE TOOL CHEST shown from a side view. G – $350.00, Ex/M – $400.00.*

PLATE 40 - *MICKEY MOUSE DIXON STUDENT SET shows a graphic scene of Mickey and Donald skiing. G – $150.00, Ex/M – $175.00.*

PLATE 41 - MICKEY MOUSE CRIB TOY is made of composition and has wire arms and legs. It was produced by the Paradise Company. G – $200.00, Ex/M – $225.00.

PLATE 42 - MICKEY MOUSE PARTY FAVORS was produced for the French marketplace and was made in Paris. Different surprises were included in each package. G – $50.00, Ex/M – $55.00.

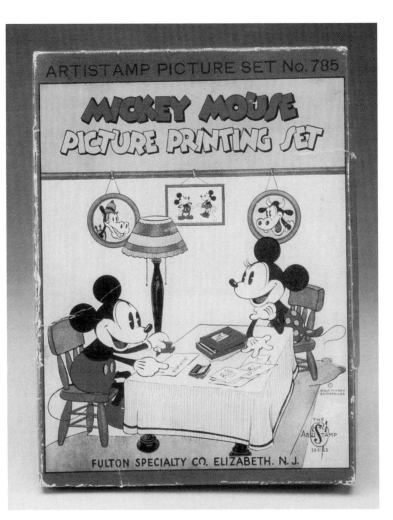

PLATE 43 - *MICKEY MOUSE PICTURE PRINT-ING SET was made by the Fulton Specialty Co. This set utilized stamps and an ink pad and was part of the Artistamp series. G – $125.00, Ex/M – $135.00.*

PLATE 44 - *MICKEY MOUSE KEYSTONE PROJECTOR shown here with a different box variation and a Cine Art film that is used with this projector. G – $350.00, Ex/M – $425.00.*

PLATE 45 - *MICKEY MOUSE POCKET WATCH BOX is marked Walt Disney. G – $200.00, Ex/M – $210.00.*

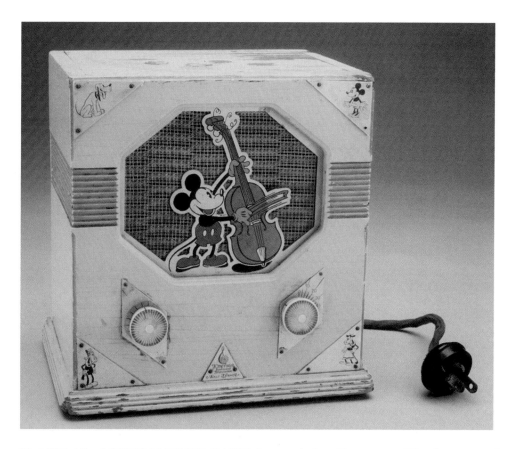

PLATE 46 - *MICKEY MOUSE RADIO is made by Emerson. The four metal plates show Mickey, Minnie, Horace Horsecollar, and Clarabelle, the Cow. G – $2,500.00, Ex/M – $3,000.00.*

PLATE 47 - MICKEY MOUSE
BATON is wood with a composi-
tion Mickey head. G – $500.00,
Ex/M – $525.00.

PLATE 48 - MICKEY MOUSE PENCIL
HOLDER was produced by the Dixon
Company. It is made of composition. G –
$300.00, Ex/M – $325.00.

**PLATE 49** - *MICKEY AND MINNIE MOUSE FIGURINES are made of bisque and are 5½" tall. It is important to make sure bisque figurines have not been repainted as it lowers their value greatly. G – $400.00, Ex/M – $450.00.*

**PLATE 50** - *MICKEY MOUSE BRACELET employs the very early rat faced Mickey.G – $150.00, Ex/M – $175.00.*

**PLATE 51** - *MICKEY MOUSE SCHOOL SALE SIGN used to advertise the Dixon pencil boxes. G – $50.00, Ex/M – $75.00.*

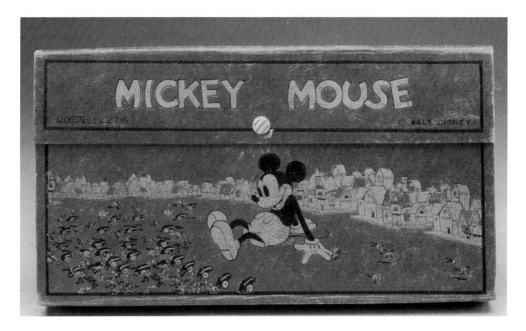

PLATE 52 - *MICKEY MOUSE PENCIL BOX. G – $100.00, Ex/M – $125.00.*

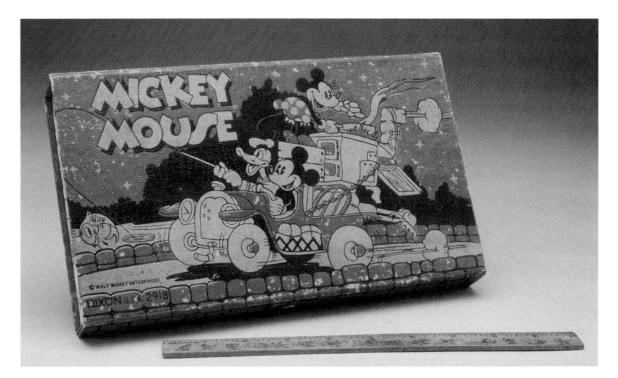

PLATE 53 - *MICKEY MOUSE PENCIL BOX is included with ruler found in all pencil boxes. G – $100.00, Ex/M – $125.00.*

PLATE 54 - *MICKEY MOUSE DIXON PENCIL BOX. G – $110.00, Ex/M – $120.00.*

PLATE 55 - *MICKEY MOUSE PENCIL BOX. G – $115.00, Ex/M – $125.00.*

PLATE 56 - *MICKEY MOUSE PENCIL BOX. G – $100.00, Ex/M – $125.00.*

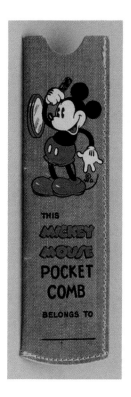

PLATE 57 - *MICKEY MOUSE POCKET COMB is marked "W.D." G – $100.00, Ex/M – $110.00.*

PLATE 58 - *MICKEY MOUSE BAND LEADER DOLL was manufactured by the Knickerbocker Toy Company. The wooden baton is included. The shoes are made of composition. G – $600.00, Ex/M – $650.00.*

**PLATE 59** - *MICKEY MOUSE NIGHT LIGHT was made by Price and is a candle surrounded by a paper label. G – $350.00, Ex/M – $400.00.*

**PLATE 60** - *MICKEY MOUSE SILVER PLATE CUP was produced by the International Silver Company. They were given as baby gifts in the 1930's. G – $225.00, Ex/M – $300.00.*

**PLATE 61** - *MICKEY MOUSE RUBBER FIGURE was made by the Seiberling Latex Rubber Company. G – $150.00, Ex/M – $175.00.*

PLATE 62 - *MICKEY MOUSE RULER is made of wood and was a give-away from the Yoo Hoo Ice Cream Cone Company. G – $50.00, Ex/M – $65.00.*

PLATE 63 - *MICKEY MOUSE PENCIL HOLDER was made by the Dixon Company and is the only figural cardbord Mickey Mouse holder made. G – $300.00, Ex/M – $325.00.*

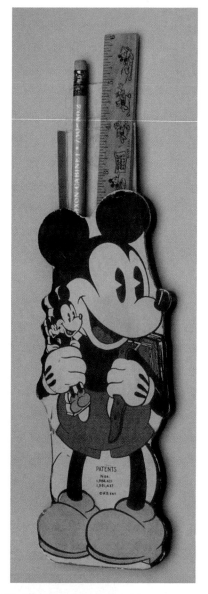

PLATE 64 - *MICKEY MOUSE PENCIL AND RULER found in the Mickey Mouse pencil box. G – $75.00, Ex/M – $85.00.*

**PLATE 65** - *MICKEY MOUSE CAMERA was manufactured by the Ensign Company in England. This box type camera is from the 1930's. G – $275.00, Ex/M – $325.00.*

**PLATE 66** - *MICKEY MOUSE WATERING CAN was made by the Ohio Art Company. G – $150.00, Ex/M – $175.00.*

PLATE 67 - *MICKEY MOUSE TARGET GAME was made by the Marks Company. The metal gun and rubber darts are also shown. G – $350.00, Ex/M – $375.00.*

PLATE 68 - *MICKEY MOUSE DRUM depicts the Mickey Mouse band and was made by the Ohio Art Company. The original wooden wooden drumsticks are also pictured. G – $400.00, Ex/M – $425.00.*

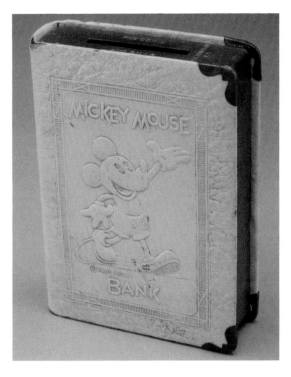

PLATE 69 - *MICKEY MOUSE BOOK BANK was made by the Dell Company and came with a small metal key. G – $100.00, Ex/M – $110.00.*

PLATE 70 - *MICKEY MOUSE AND MINNIE MOUSE MILITARY BISQUE SET. G – $350.00, Ex/M – $450.00.*

PLATE 71 - *MICKEY MOUSE BABY TOY is made of celluloid. G – $200.00, Ex/M – $225.00.*

PLATE 72 - *MICKEY MOUSE CHILD'S POTTY is made of porcelain over metal. Walt Disney himself gave these as baby presents. They came in various colors. G – $350.00, Ex/M – $375.00.*

**PLATE 73** - *MICKEY MOUSE WOODEN PULL TOY was made by the Chad Valley Company in England. G – $400.00, Ex/M – $425.00.*

**PLATE 74** - *MICKEY MOUSE FRENCH HORN BISQUE is 5½" tall. G – $500.00, Ex/M – $525.00.*

**PLATE 75** - *MINNIE MOUSE FUN-E-FLEX figure is made of wood. The flowers attached to the hat are almost impossible to find. G – $300.00, Ex/M – $325.00.*

PLATE 76 - *MICKEY MOUSE MUSICIANS are made of celluloid and each holds a different musical instrument. G – $200.00, Ex/M – $250.00.*

PLATE 77 - *MICKEY MOUSE PARTY HORN was made by Marks Brothers and is a heavy cardboard with a wooden mouth piece. G – $75.00, Ex/M – $85.00.*

PLATE 78 - MICKEY MOUSE ASHTRAY is made of metal. G – $400.00, Ex/M – $425.00.

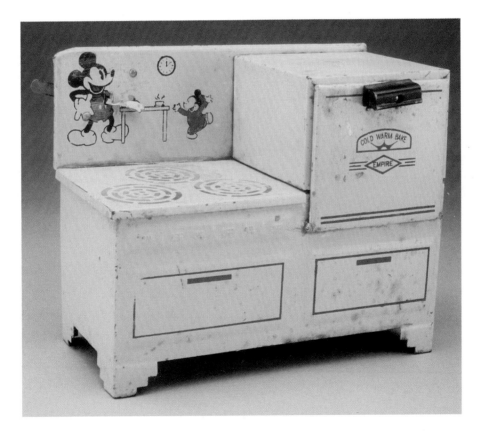

PLATE 79 - MICKEY MOUSE STOVE is made by the Empire Company. The stove is metal. G – $600.00, Ex/M – $650.00.

**PLATE 80** - *MICKEY MOUSE STOVE is made by the Empire Company and is the electric version. G – $600.00, Ex/M – $650.00.*

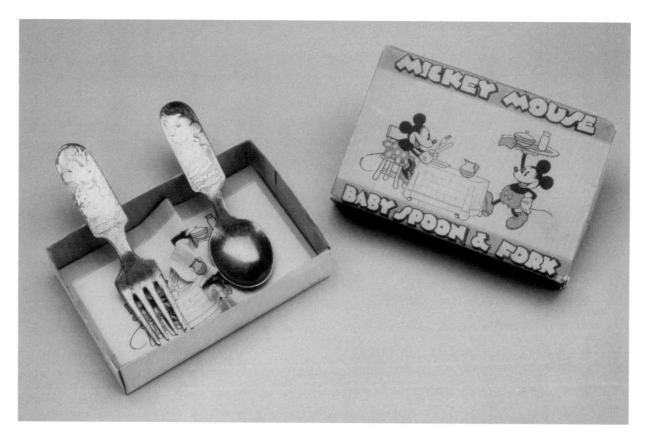

**PLATE 81** - *MICKEY MOUSE BABY SPOON & FORK SET was given as a baby gift. The spoon and fork are stainless steel. G – $300.00, Ex/M – $350.00.*

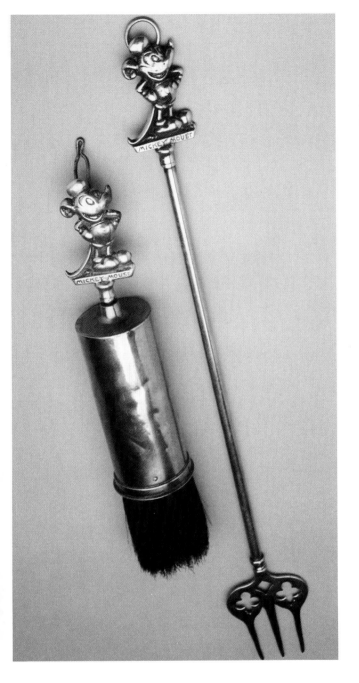

PLATE 82 - *MICKEY MOUSE FIREPLACE ACCES-SORIES are made of metal. G – $400.00, Ex/M – $425.00.*

PLATE 83 - *MICKEY MOUSE DOLL was produced by the Knickerbocker Toy Company. G – $500.00, Ex/M – $525.00.*

**PLATE 84 - MICKEY MOUSE CONTAINER** *was made of a glazed ceramic produced in Germany. G – $300.00, Ex/M – $325.00.*

**PLATE 85 - MICKEY MOUSE ASHTRAY** *was made of ceramic with a wobbly spring-legged fiddler Mickey. G – $400.00, Ex/M – $425.00.*

**PLATE 86 - MICKEY MOUSE CANES** *utilized Fun-E-Flex Mickey heads as the cane tops. G – $300.00, Ex/M – $325.00.*

**PLATE 87** - *MICKEY MOUSE LAPEL WATCH was produced by Ingersoll and is one of the rarest of all early watches. G – $900.00, Ex/M – $1,000.00.*

**PLATE 88** - *MICKEY MOUSE LAPEL WATCH had a paper decal on the back that is hard to find in good condition. G – $900.00, Ex/M – $1,000.00.*

**PLATE 89** - *MICKEY MOUSE CANDY TIN was European and shows the early rat-faced Mickey. G – $350.00, Ex/M – $450.00.*

**PLATE 90** - *MICKEY MOUSE BUBBLE BUSTER was made by the Kilgore Company. The gun shot little pellets. The gun is made of metal. G – $500.00, Ex/M – $525.00.*

PLATE 91 - *MICKEY MOUSE COLORED PENCILS. G – $150.00, Ex/M – $175.00.*

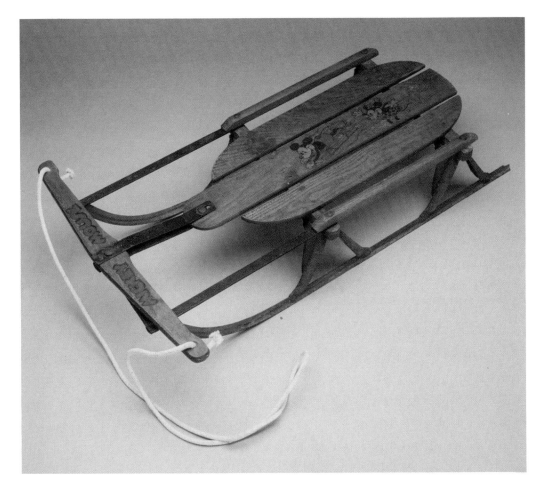

PLATE 92 - *MICKEY MOUSE SLED was used by children in the 1930's. The condition of the decal is essential in determining value. G – $500.00, Ex/M – $550.00.*

PLATE 93 - *MICKEY MOUSE BANJO PLAYER BISQUE. G – $525.00, Ex/M – $550.00.*

PLATE 94 - *ROCKING HORSE MICK-EY MOUSE is one of the few hand-painted wooden windups featuring Mickey Mouse. G – $2,000.00, Ex/M – $2,500.00.*

PLATE 95 - *MICKEY MOUSE ASHTRAY is made of glazed ceramic. G – $225.00, Ex/M – $275.00.*

**PLATE 96** - *MICKEY MOUSE COWBOY DOLL is made by the Knickerbocker Toy Company. The hat, kerchief, rope, chaps and holsters are essential parts of this doll. G – $1,500.00, Ex/M – $1,800.00.*

**PLATE 97** - *MINNIE MOUSE COWGIRL DOLL is the companion piece to Plate 95. The shoes are made of composition. G – $1,500.00, Ex/M – $1,800.00.*

PLATE 98 - *CERAMIC CUP AND SAUCER are pieces of Bavarian china. G – $300.00, Ex/M – $350.00.*

PLATE 99 - *BAVARIAN CHINA MARKINGS. G – $300.00, Ex/M – $350.00.*

**PLATE 100** - *MICKEY MOUSE DEAN'S RAG DOLL was produced in England. G – $375.00, Ex/M – $425.00.*

**PLATE 101** - *MICKEY MOUSE KNICKERBOCKER DOLL with original hang tag. G – $900.00, Ex/M – $925.00.*

PLATE 102 - *MINNIE MOUSE KNICKERBOCK-ER DOLL with original hang tag. G – $900.00, Ex/M – $925.00.*

PLATE 103 - *MICKEY MOUSE POST OFFICE BANK was made by the Happynak Company of England. G – $75.00, Ex/M – $125.00.*

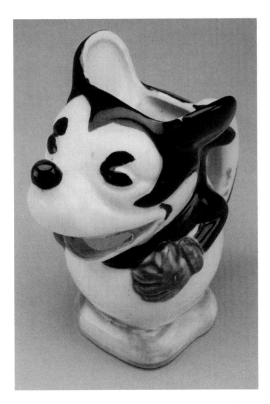

PLATE 105 - *MICKEY MOUSE PERFUME BOTTLE was made of a glazed ceramic in Germany. G – $450.00, Ex/M – $500.00.*

PLATE 104 - *MICKEY MOUSE CREAMER was made of glazed ceramic. G – $250.00, Ex/M – $275.00.*

PLATE 106 - *MICKEY MOUSE LAMP was produced by the Soreng-Manegold Company. The original shade is very tough to find. G – $1,800.00, Ex/M – $2,200.00.*

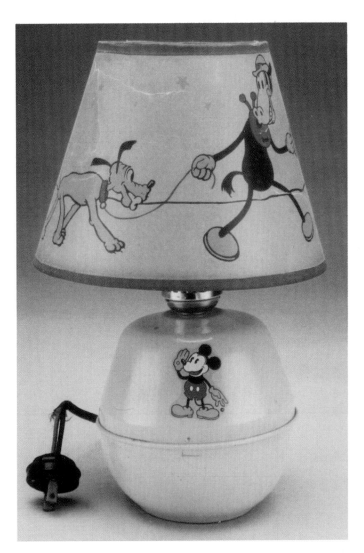

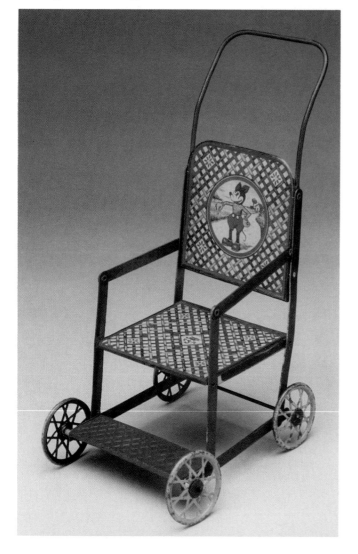

PLATE 107 - MICKEY MOUSE STROLLER *was made by the RSA Company in Spain. The stroller is tin. G – $750.00, Ex/M – $950.00.*

PLATE 108 - MICKEY MOUSE EXPRESS TRAIN *is made of wood and was produced in England. G – $650.00, Ex/M – $700.00.*

PLATE 109 - *MICKEY MOUSE UMBRELLA is made of fabric with a plastic Pluto handle. G - $120.00, Ex/M - $125.00.*

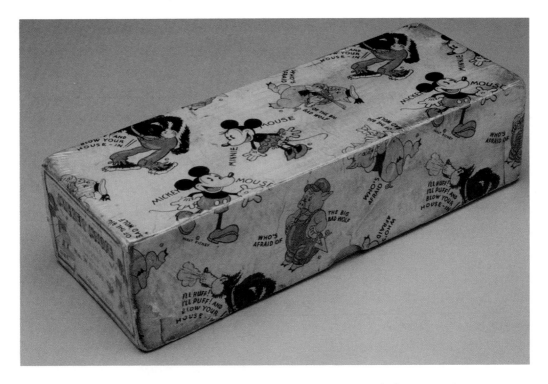

PLATE 110 - *MICKEY MOUSE HOSE SUPPORTER made by A. Stein & Company. G – $200.00, Ex/M – $225.00.*

PLATE 111 - *MICKEY MOUSE POST TOASTIES CEREAL BOX was made in the 1930's and is impossible to find in this condition. G – $600.00, Ex/M – $650.00.*

PLATE 112 - *MICKEY MOUSE JEWELRY SET is shown on original cards in the original box. G – $1,800.00, Ex/M – $2,000.00.*

PLATE 113 - *MICKEY MOUSE OLD MAID GAME utilized all the Disney characters on the old maid cards. G – $50.00, Ex/M – $75.00.*

PLATE 114 - *MICKEY MOUSE, MINNIE MOUSE, AND PLUTO are all Fun-E-Flex figures. They are the larger sizes. Note the four fingered hands and original tails. G – $1,200.00, Ex/M – $1,400.00 each.*

**PLATE 115** - *MICKEY MOUSE BLACKBOARD was manufactured by the Falcon Company. G – $150.00, Ex/M – $175.00.*

PLATE 116 - *MICKEY MOUSE BLACK-BOARD was produced by the Rich-mond School Furniture Company of Muncie, Indiana. G – $300.00, Ex/M – $325.00.*

PLATE 117 - *MICKEY MOUSE SCATTER BALL GAME is the English version made by Chad Valley Games. G – $300.00, Ex/M – $325.00.*

PLATE 118 - *MICKEY MOUSE BOXED TEA SET is made of lusterware glazed ceramic. G – $550.00, Ex/M – $600.00.*

PLATE 119 - *MICKEY MOUSE HOT WATER BOTTLE was used as a baby present. G – $310.00, Ex/M – $325.00.*

**PLATE 120** - *MINNIE MOUSE TOOTH-BRUSH HOLDER is made of bisque and has one movable arm. Shown with its original figural toothbrush. G – $400.00, Ex/M – $425.00.*

**PLATE 121** - *MICKEY MOUSE SILVER BOWL. G – $200.00, Ex/M – $250.00.*

PLATE 122 - *MICKEY MOUSE SILVER MUG was made by the International Silver Company. G – $150.00, Ex/M – $200.00.*

PLATE 123 - *MICKEY MOUSE METAL BANK was produced for the English market. G – $400.00, Ex/M – $450.00.*

PLATE 124 - *MICKEY MOUSE TELEPHONE was made by the Hill Brass Company. Mickey Mouse is made of hard cardboard and pops up when the handset is picked up. G – $400.00, Ex/M – $450.00.*

PLATE 126 - MICKEY MOUSE BAYARD CLOCK BOX is from the 1930's French clock. Now all that is needed is the 1930's clock. G – $200.00, Ex/M – $225.00.

PLATE 125 - MICKEY MOUSE MOVIE PROJECTOR FILMS were used by the movie-jector. Each set came with six separate films. G – $300.00, Ex/M – $325.00.

PLATE 127 - MICKEY MOUSE RACE CAR is mechanical and measures 3". They came in a variety of colors. G – $375.00, Ex/M – $425.00.

# Long-billed Donald

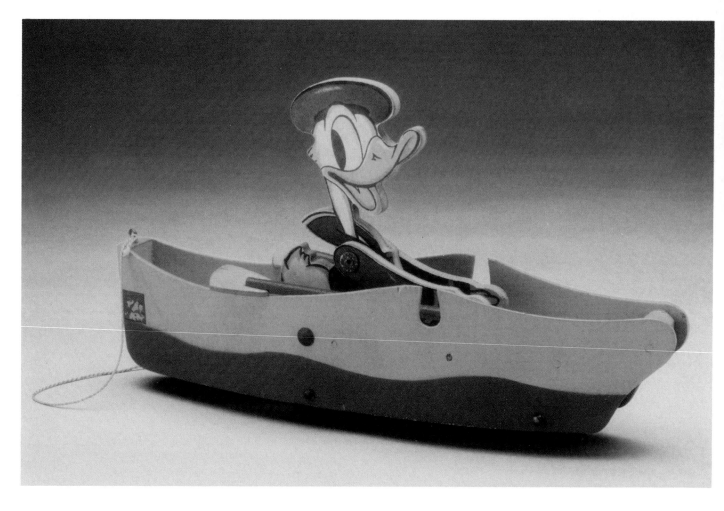

Although Mickey and Minnie Mouse were considered Walt Disney's leading man and lady (or leading mice!) in the early 1930's, the Disney studio quicky realized that simple plots based around two mice and a single villain would be too thin. So very shortly after the creation of Mickey and Minnie Mouse in the late 1920's, an interesting ensemble of other characters emerged from the Disney stable. First appearing were Pluto the Pup, Clarabelle Cow, Horace Horsecollar, and Dippy the Goof, later to be known as simply Goofy. The last of the major Disney comic characters to enter the movie scene was Donald Duck, who didn't appear on the screen or in toy merchandising until 1934. Prior to that time, nearly all of the early Disney character items would picture Mickey, Minnie, Pluto, Horace, Dippy, and Clarabelle. If Donald is missing from the design of the item, it is a good bet the toy is pre-1935.

All of the Disney comic characters afforded studio artists the chance to expand plot lines, gags, and movie bits to include a greater variety of action and story possibilities. Because each animal's personality was built around certain character traits of his particular species, these new characters opened up the gate on a stampede of barnyard humor in the early films.

The Disney studios utilized the awkward lankiness of Horace Horsecollar and the somewhat homely clumsiness of Clarabelle Cow to their best advantage. No matter how they drew here or what she wore, Clarabelle was never pretty. But we loved her for what she was — a cow! And Pluto was a peculiar oddity since the studio chose to present him as a smaller companion to Mickey Mouse. In most early illustrations and merchandise, Mickey and Minnie were presented as about two-thirds the height of Horace and Clarabelle. Since the mouse-to-horse and mouse-to-cow scale was already totally unrealistic, Disney artists were free to draw Pluto as Mickey's shorter companion. However, it should be noted, on a few of the early Japanese celluloid Mickey Mouse and Pluto toys, Mickey is presented as a much smaller creature as compared to Pluto (See Chapter One).

But regardless of the popularity of the early characters of Horace, Clarabelle, Dippy, and Pluto, none could claim the real title of supporting actor from Donald Duck. Aside from Mickey and Minnie, Donald was the most developed character of the Walt Disney Studios. Donald played the frustrated, volatile, unfortunate clown to Mickey Mouse's straight man, or mouse. If an early Oscar would have been given to the best actor/animation character in the 1930's, it should certainly have gone to Donald Duck. Although we may never have realized it, Donald's temperamental personality brought a very human dimension to the cartoon screen. He was the little guy who always got the pie in the face, the webbed foot squashed, the bill smashed, or was generally outsmarted. In a sense, he was us. And we laughed at him and cheered for him. On the screen, Donald brought forth a unique, humorously dramatic personality something that was missing from the cartoons of competing studios in the 1930's.

It is fitting that we begin our photo section beyond Mickey and Minnie Mouse with the cartoon actor who so justly deserved at least the "Number Three" spot: Donald Duck. The Donald Duck toy designs are a beautiful complement for and contrast to the 1930's Mickey and Minnie Mouse toys. Whereas Mickey and Minnie were usually designed into toys with colors of red, yellow, black, and white, the Donald Duck toys of the 1930's picture him with bright or navy blue, lots of white, yellow, and/or bright orange. In regard to color and design, Donald is as nearly diametrically opposite of Mickey Mouse as he could possible be. This great contrast is what makes Disneyana collectors dearly love toy examples of both!

The Donald Duck Ingersol Watch pictured in Plate 128 was not even known to exist until about four years ago when one was discovered in its original box. The one found had enamel Donalds on the metal bracelet. I believe it was also made with the Mickey band pictured here. The Donald Duck Ingersol Watch is one of the rarest and hardest to find.

A very attractive celluloid Donald windup is the Donald Duck Nodder pictured in Plate 129. Although the toy utilizes a very simple elastic rubber band windup mechanism, the nodding action of the long-billed head is very humorous and fun to watch. The winking eye and long bill symbolizes the Donald Duck look of the 1930's.

Both the Donald Duck on Scooter in Plate 130 and the Donald Duck on Rocking Horse in Plate 131 are hard to find bisque figures. Anytime a Donald figure is associated with another object (paint can, tricycle, etc..) the bisque is much rarer and more valuable than a plain standing bisque figure.

An unusual Fisher-Price toy is the Donald Duck Pop-Up Paddle toy pictured in Plate 132. This is the rarest of all the paddle toys manufactured by that company and is extremely hard to find with the original wings. When the string is pulled, Donald quacks.

Pictured in Plate 133 is the Seiberling Latex Squeak Donald Duck toy. The hollow version is the rarest of the three variations because of its fragile hollow construction. Many of these examples either flattened or disintegrated over the years. Collectors should be especially aware that not all Seiberling figures stand up well even though they may appear to be in mint condition. Before purchasing such examples, always try to stand the figure up. As the hard rubber in these toys ages, it often forces the flat feet to curl upward slightly. Minor off-balance imperfections can be fixed by placing a dab of putty or a coin under the feet. Badly distorted figures should be passed up unless the collector plans to display them lying down in a case.

In Plate 134 is pictured a Donald Jack-In-The Box. Donald is celluloid with a furry bottom. When closed and Donald "pops" out a squeaking voice is emitted. Another incredible celluloid toy is pictured in Plate 135. Donald Duck On Trapeze is a rare wind up and even rarer is the bright and colorful original box.

**PLATE 128 - DONALD DUCK WATCH** *was made by the Ingersol Company and is one of a handful known to exist. It has also been seen with enamel Donald Ducks on the bracelet. G – $3,000.00, Ex/M – $3,500.00.*

**PLATE 129 - DONALD DUCK NODDER** *is made of celluloid and operated by a simple wire mechanism. Note the long bill and winking eye that characterized Donald in the 1930's. G – $1,800.00, Ex/M – $2,000.00.*

**PLATE 130 - DONALD DUCK ON SCOOTER** *is made of bisque and hand painted in Japan. G – $275.00, Ex/M – $325.00.*

PLATE 131 - *DONALD DUCK ON ROCK-ING HORSE is a bisque figure. Values are increased when an object (rocking horse) is associated with a bisque fig-urine. G – $275.00, Ex/M – $325.00.*

PLATE 132 - *DONALD DUCK POP UP PADDLE was created by Fisher-Price and is the rarest of the paddle toys. The wings are made of leather and are very difficult to find. G – $450.00, Ex/M – $500.00.*

PLATE 133 - *DONALD DUCK RUBBER SQUEAK TOY was produced by the Sieberling Latex Company. This variation is hollow and squeaks when pushed. $G – $375.00, Ex/M – $425.00.*

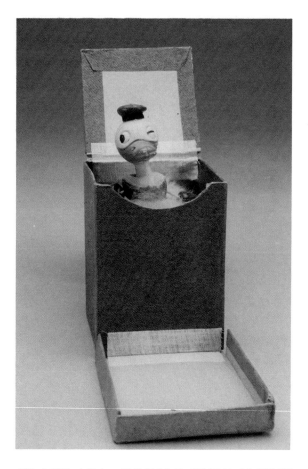

PLATE 134 - *DONALD DUCK JACK-IN-THE-BOX is made of celluloid. G – $1,000.00, Ex/M – $1,200.00*

PLATE 135 - *DONALD DUCK SAND PAIL was on example of tin lithography. It is marked Walt Disney Enterprises. G – $400.00, Ex/M – $425.00.*

PLATE 136 - *DONALD DUCK TRAPEZE is a celluloid windup toy. The bright and colorful original box enhances the value of the toy dramatically. G – $1,500.00, Ex/M – $1,800.00.*

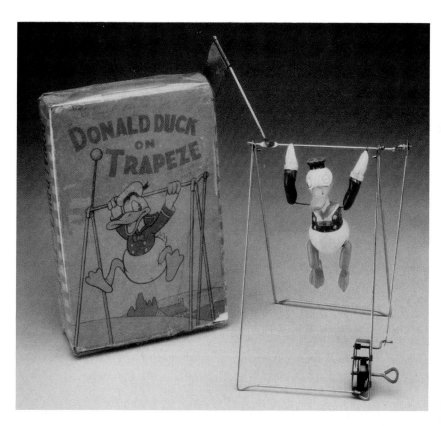

PLATE 138 - *DONALD DUCK WATERING CAN was made by the Ohio Art Company which is still in existence today. G – $175.00, Ex/M – $200.00.*

PLATE 137 - *DONALD DUCK BANK was produced by the Crown Toy Company. It is made of composition and has a moveable head. There is a metal trap door on the bottom. G – $300.00, Ex/M – $350.00.*

PLATE 139 - *DONALD DUCK CRIB TOY is composition with wire arm and legs. G – $200.00, Ex/M – $225.00.*

PLATE 140 - DONALD DUCK BEACH BAG *was made by the Skipper Company. It is a canvas-like material and marked "W.D. Enterprises." G – $200.00, Ex/M – $225.00.*

PLATE 141 - DONALD DUCK RUG *is shown with its vibrant colors. G – $240.00, Ex/M – $260.00.*

**PLATE 142** - *DONALD DUCK CHILD'S FEEDING DISH was utilized by parents to keep their children's food hot. G – $75.00, Ex/M – $80.00.*

**PLATE 143** - *DONALD DUCK DRUM was made by the Ohio Art Company. The drum is metal. G – $150.00, Ex/M – $200.00.*

PLATE 144 - *DONALD DUCK SOAP was produced by the Lightfoot Schultz Company and contained a figural Donald. G – $175.00, Ex/M – $200.00.*

PLATE 145 - *DONALD DUCK PENCIL BOX was made by Dixon and shown here with the ruler that came with the set. G – $110.00, Ex/M – $125.00.*

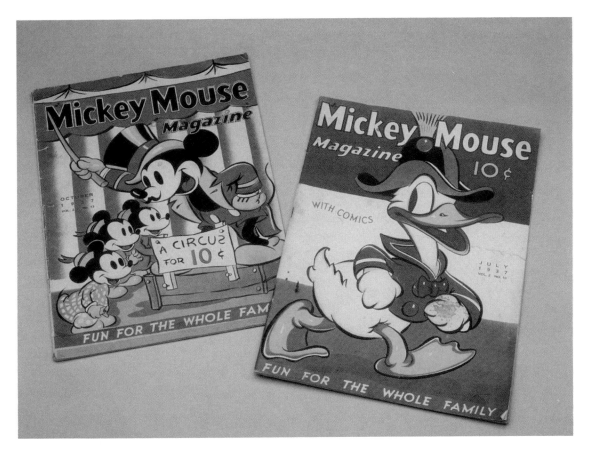

PLATE 146 - *DONALD DUCK MAGAZINE cover that sold for $.10 in 1937. G – $35.00, Ex/M – $40.00.*

PLATE 147 - *DONALD DUCK PIN BACK BUTTON shown here advertising the Norwich Knitting Company. G – $300.00, Ex/M – $350.00.*

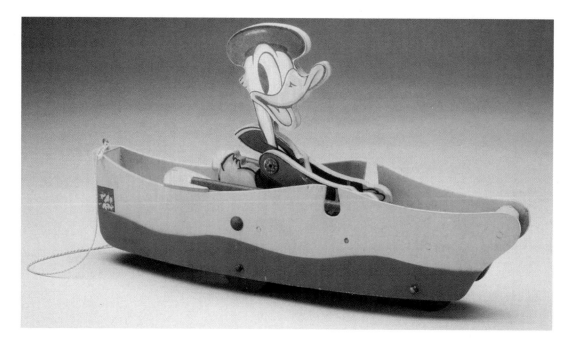

PLATE 148 - *DONALD DUCK PULL TOY was made by Chad Valley Company in England. The boat is made of wood. G – $400.00, Ex/M – $425.00.*

PLATE 149 - *DONALD DUCK WATERING CAN. G – $175.00, Ex/M – $185.00.*

PLATE 150 - *DONALD DUCK TRACTOR was made by the Sun Rubber Company. It is harder to find than the Mickey Mouse version. G – $175.00, Ex/M – $190.00.*

PLATE 151 - *DONALD DUCK LANTERN was made in England by Johnson of Hendon and is marked "Walt Disney - Mickey Mouse LTD." G – $200.00, Ex/M – $210.00.*

# Friends from the Golden Age

Walt Disney may have founded and financed his studio on the popularity of Mickey Mouse in the 1930's, but it was his unique experimentation with the featurette and feature length cartoon that put the Walt Disney Studio on the map as a viable Hollywood entity. No one can speculate exactly what would have happened had the Disney Studio chosen to continue producing cartoon shorts only. Mickey Mouse might have become old hat. The studio might have lost its creative edge. Fortunately for Disneyana collectors, Walt chose to set his sights on a larger goal than simply the production of one popular Mickey Mouse cartoon after another. Historians have called Walt Disney a visionary. Animation film experts have called him a genius. And most Disneyana collectors look up to him with a friendly admiration and a childlike awe and simply call him Walt. Though we may not own his autograph, nor ever have been fortunate enough to shake his hand, he seems our friend; almost family. And it was his creation of the countless Disney feature films that taught us the real spectacle of fairy tales. It is this sense of awe, this endearment,

that drives today's Disneyana collectors through countless toy shows and flea markets searching for remembrances of those Saturday afternoon matinees filled with wicked witches, beautiful princesses, seven little dwarfs, a wooden puppet who dances without strings, and of course, Mickey Mouse.

Film animation underwent a unique evolution at the Walt Disney Studios in the 1930's. Walt knew that animation could make a greater impact on the movie world than simply filling the open time slots between feature films and the refreshment stand. But the studio did not jump immediately from the Mickey Mouse short cartoons to the feature length animation films. There was a logical progression. "The Silly Symphonies" were short subject films which had no unifying character from one film to the next. Neither did they have any unifying theme. From "Flowers and Trees," the world's first color cartoon, to "Three Little Pigs," the "Silly Symphonies" allowed Walt and his studio to experiment with special effects, new animation techniques, color animation, and the relationship of animation to the other most important aspects of the film experience, music and sound. These "Symphonies" then, were stepping stones to the experimental full-length animation feature project, *Snow White and the Seven Dwarfs.*

One of the most popular of all the Disney short animation films was "Three Little Pigs," which appeared in 1933. Because America had only recently slipped into the grasp of the Great Depression, this little film with its unlikely heroes became something of a national symbol as the little guy attempted to hold off the Big Bad Wolf. The famous song, "Who's Afraid of the Big Bad Wolf," made its debut in the film and was a hit not only because of its catchy tune and tie-in to the story, but also because it symbolized American triumph and bravery in hard times. Therefore, aside from Mickey and Minnie Mouse, Three Little Pigs collectibles are some of the earliest Walt Disney Enterprises' pieces.

After *Snow White and the Seven Dwarfs* in 1937 and *Ferdinand the Bull* in 1938; the Walt Disney Studios brought forth what many Disneyana fans and animation film critics believe was Disney's most artistically perfect animated feature of all time, *Pinocchio.* Although *Snow White* may have been dearest in the hearts of Walt Disney and his original artists because it was their first feature, *Pinocchio* was by far their most beautiful work. The color, the spectacle, the smooth animation sequences including the human Geppetto, the absolutely miraculous animation backgrounds, the experimentation with interesting camera angles and zooming, and the dynamic strength of characterization all combined to make Pinocchio an animation history milestone that has never really been surpassed. And if ever there was a character who virtually cried out to be mass produced into toys, it

was Walt Disney's Pinocchio! Consider this: Pinocchio was first a puppet, then half puppet and half boy. The combination of these qualities helped him to become one of the best loved of all the 1940's Disney characters. Toy designers under the authorization of the Walt Disney Studio had a heyday with Pinocchio. For the first time, they had an actual puppet character to adapt to the puppet toys. And the results were nothing short of spectacular!

Walt Disney's *Pinocchio* rounded out the 1930's for the studio. Pinocchio was released in February 1940, but some of the merchandise has a 1939 copyright date because Disney wanted to get the merchandise on the shelves before the film was released. These items, and all items manufactured after late 1939 until 1940, are marked with the "new" copyright notice, "Walt Disney Productions." Toys after Pinocchio will never have the "Walt Disney Enterprises" copyright notice. With this final, significant film of a momentous Hollywood decade, the Walt Disney Studio began to turn the corner toward a new, modern era, the fabulous Forties. No one knew how soon the world would be at war, but the optimism and youthfulness that Walt Dlsney's film animation and toys had brought the nation would be cherished forever. As the song "When You Wish Upon A Star" surfaced as a symbol for not only the film *Pinocchio* but for the Disney Studio itself, Americans looked up to the heavens and into their hearts for the peace and dreams of their youth.

The peace of the moment was soon to end. But the childhood dreams of "When You Wish Upon A Star" would endure. Walt Disney would see to that.

To start off the Friends from the Golden Age Chapter pictured in Plate 152 is a beautiful Snow White and Seven Dwarfs Bisque Set in its original box. Each dwarf was hand painted in Japan. There were different sizes produced.

Pictured in Plate 153 is a Who's Afraid of the Big Bad Wolf bank referred to as a book bank. It is complete with original box and key so when enough money was saved it could be retrieved without breaking the bank.

The Elmer the Elephant Seiberling Latex Rubber Figure shown in Plate 154 is very hard to find in good condition. It was not unusual for the sun to melt these rubber figurines. Elmer's head is movable.

Two of my favorite pieces are the wooden Fun-E-Flex Horace Horsecollars found in Plate 155. Horace merchandise is very scarce and these two variations are almost complete and both tails are original.

Plate 156 shows the rarest version of the Snow White and the Seven Dwarfs bisque set. The musical instrument set is much harder to find and also more desirable.

PLATE 152 - *SNOW WHITE AND THE SEVEN DWARFS BOXED BISQUE SET was made and hand printed in Japan. G – $600.00, Ex/M – $650.00.*

PLATE 153 - *WHO'S AFRAID OF THE BIG BAD WOLF BANK is referred to as a book bank and is made of leatherette material. G – $300.00, Ex/M – $350.00.*

PLATE 154 - *ELMER THE ELEPHANT RUBBER FIGURE was made by the Sieberling Latex Rubber Company. The head is movable. G – $300.00, Ex/M – $350.00.*

PLATE 155 - *HORACE HORSECOLLAR WOODEN FIGURES were made by the Fun-E-Flex Company. They are very different and each is very rare. G – $1,300.00, Ex/M – $1,500.00.*

PLATE 156 - SNOW WHITE AND THE SEVEN DWARFS BOXED BISQUE SET *is the rarer set with each dwarf carrying a different musical instrument.* G – $600.00, Ex/M – $675.00.

PLATE 157 - SNOW WHITE AND THE SEVEN DWARFS DRESS BUTTON SET *made by the Hollywood Company.* G – $40.00, Ex/M – $50.00.

PLATE 158 - *CLARABELLE THE COW BISCUIT TIN was made in France in the 1930's. G – $450.00, Ex/M – $500.00.*

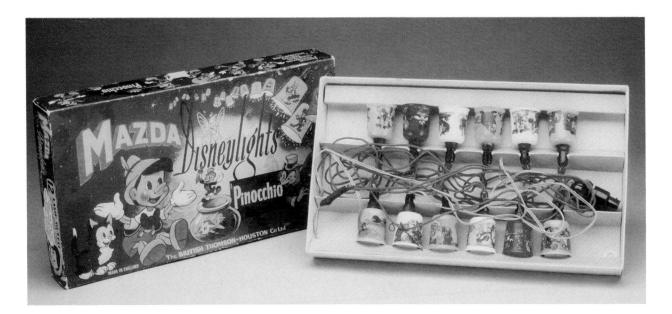

PLATE 159 - *DISNEYLIGHTS were made in England by Thomson-Houston Company, Ltd. The lampshades are made of plastic and each shows a different scene from the movie. G – $300.00, Ex/M – $325.00.*

PLATE 161 - *RUBBER THREE LITTLE PIGS are hard to find in good condition because most of them melted. G – $350.00, Ex/M – $350.00.*

PLATE 160 - *SIEBERLING LATEX RUBBER THREE LITTLE PIGS are hollow. G – $300.00, Ex/M – $350.00.*

PLATE 162 - *FIDDLER PIG completes the set of three. G – $300.00, Ex/M – $350.00.*

PLATE 163 - *HORACE HORSECOLLAR CRIB TOY is made of composition with wire arms and legs. G – $200.00, Ex/M – $250.00.*

PLATE 164 - *CLARABELLE THE COW PENCIL BOX made by Dixon and marked "Walt Disney Enterprises." G – $100.00, Ex/M – $110.00.*

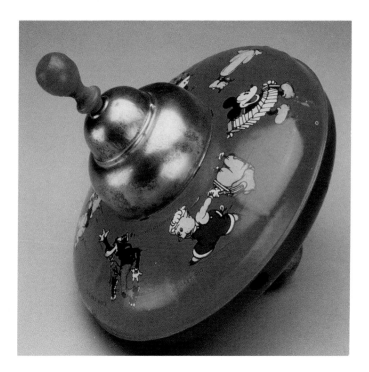

**PLATE 165 - *THREE LITTLE PIGS SPIN-
NING TOP is made of metal. G – $175.00,
Ex/M – $200.00.***

**PLATE 166 - *SNOW WHITE AND THE SEVEN DWARFS LIGHT SET made by Noma. Box insert
enhances value greatly. G – $300.00, Ex/M – $325.00.***

**PLATE 167 - THREE LIT-TLE PIGS SPOON AND FORK BOAT** *made by the William Rogers & Son Company and was given as a child's gift in the 1930's. G – $200.00, Ex/M – $225.00.*

**PLATE 168 - DOPEY LAMP** *made by the La Mode Company, shown here with original hard to find shade. $G – $175.00, Ex/M – $200.00.*

PLATE 169 - *DISNEY CHAR-ACTER BLOCKS featuring Horace Horsecollar,Clarabelle the Cow, and Goofy. They are mode of wood. G – $180.00, Ex/M – $190.00.*

PLATE 170 - *THE THREE PALS BISQUE SET made in Japan. Shown here in mint 100% paint condition. G – $800.00, Ex/M – $950.00.*

**PLATE 171-** *DISNEYLAND SAFETY BLOCKS were made by the American Company and each displayed a famous Disney character. G – $175.00, Ex/M – $190.00.*

**PLATE 172 -** *PLUTO DRESS BUTTONS made by the Hollywood Company. G – $40.00, Ex/M – $45.00.*

PLATE 173 - FUN-E-FLEX PLUTO THE PUP shown here with wooden doghouse that is hard to find. G – $200.00, Ex/M – $250.00.

PLATE 174 - ELMER THE ELEPHANT BISQUE was produced in Japan. The trunk is movable. G – $450.00, Ex/M – $475.00.

PLATE 175 - BIG BAD WOLF BOX made for the Seiberling Latex Company. I have yet to find the wolf that goes in the box. $G – $300.00, Ex/M – $325.00.

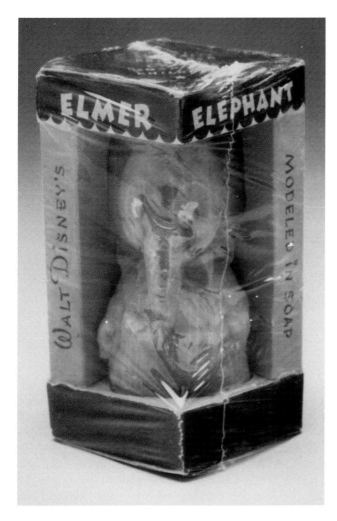

PLATE 176 - *ELMER THE ELEPHANT SOAP found in its original packaging. G – $150.00, Ex/M – $175.00.*

PLATE 177 - *THREE LITTLE PIGS ASHTRAYS are made of glazed ceramic and referred to as luster ware. G – $200.00, Ex/M – $225.00.*

# Disneyana of the 1940's, 1950's, and 1960's

Although most collectors of Disneyana today would agree that the true "Golden Age" of Disney character toy production was the 1930's, most would also agree that the l940's, 1950's, and 1960's also saw the production of many unique, interesting, and valuable Disney toys. From the rare and unusual Occupied Japan celluloid windup toys pictured at the beginning of this chapter to the more common dime- store toys pictured throughout this section, the supply and variety of items produced under the authorization of the Walt Disney Studios during these three decades seems almost endless. And although many collectors like to focus on Disneyana collectibles from the 1930's, it is the collectibles from the 1940's, 1950's, and 1960's that are increasing in value sometimes at almost astronomical rates! The decade of the 1940's brought an admiring public *Pinocchio, Fantasia, Bambi, Dumbo, The Three Caballeros, Song of the South,* and a host of short Mickey Mouse and Donald Duck cartoons. The 1950's saw the production of *Cinderella, Alice in Wonderland, Peter Pan, Lady and the Tramp,* and *Sleeping Beauty.* The 1950's also represent a very significant period of branching out for the Walt Disney Studio, with the opening of the world-famous Disneyland. The advent of Disneyland and America's love affair with the new electronic medium of television are both unique milestones in the popular and cultural history of the 1950's in this country. The Mickey Mouse Club also appeared as a now classic early television production during this decade. All across America on school day afternoons, youngsters sat in front of the small oval

black and white picture tubes mesmerized by early Mickey cartoons, Mouseketeers, and of course, Annette. Days of such sheer simplicity, splendor, and fun are not soon to be forgotten. That is why the Disneyana collectibles from the 1950's are treasured so dearly by a whole generation of Mouseketeers—to keep the Mickey Mouse Club alive! The 1960's brought with them the flourishing of Disneyland, "Walt Disney's Wonderful World of Color" as a spectacular Sunday evening television show brought out just when color TV was becoming popular, and a host of new animated features. *One Hundred and One Dalmations,The Jungle Book, The Sword in the Stone,* and, of course, the live action hit *Mary Poppins* all appeared during this decade. Plans for a new super Disney theme park in central Florida began to take shape, and before it could be complete, the world would lose the maker of the mouse.

It is ironic that with the death of Walt Disney in 1966, the Pop-Art revolution of the mid-1960's began to thrust comic art and character watches once again into the limelight. Walt Disney never really got to see how crazy people could get over collecting the early Disney memorabilia. As with any great artist, it is almost as if the memorabilia wasn't really collectible until we lost Walt. After his death, we all scrambled for some tangible way to hang on to those earlier, carefree, childhood Disney days. And scramble we did, for many of the nation's leading Disneyana collectors have now been at it for almost 30 years. Although these "old guys" who have amassed absolutely phenomenal collections got in when the going was good and even rare pieces didn't cost them an arm and a leg, there is still plenty of good Disney memorabilia available on the market to satisfy even the novice collector. And collecting Disneyana from the 1940's, 1950's, and 1960's is a logical place to start.

Pictured in Plate 178 is one of a series of sought-after birthday watches. The Bambi Birthday Watch is one of a set of six. The luminous pen accompanied the watch. All birthday watches come in the box pictured here.

In Plate 179 and Plate 180 is Donald Duck Drummer a tin wind up produced by Linemar. Tin windups are very hard to find in near mint condition. Beware, rust lowers the price dramatically. Conversely the original boxes of the tin windups can double sometimes triple the value of the wind up.

In Plate 181 is a Donald Duck Ceramic bank by the Leeds China Company. Leeds was responsible for an array of glazed ceramic Disney character planters, banks, figurines, cookie jars, and salt and pepper shakers brought to the market in the 1940's and 1950's. Although these were easily found in abundant supply less than ten years ago, their increasing popularity and skyrocketing value has made them one of the most economically volatile collectible items of the past two years.

Fisher-Price Toys like the Donald Duck and Nephews pictured in Plate 182 are widely sought after. Any Fisher-Price wood pull toy has gone up in value. The earlier the vintage, the more the piece is worth.

Plate 183 has Snow White and the Seven Dwarfs Disneykin set made by Marx and shown in their individual boxes. Disneykins though produced in the 1970's have fast become a "hot" newer Disneyana collectible.

The Dopey Ceramic Planter in Plate 184 is another example of Leeds China Company ceramic.

The Helbros backward Goofy Watch shown here in Plate 185 is one of the most sought after later vintage watch. The watch was produced recently as a limited edition collector's item. When first produced, there was a limited run as the idea of a watch going backwards was not embraced by the consumer.

The Snow White and the Seven Dwarfs Goebel set as shown in Plate 186 is very rare. The stylized Bee marking means it was made in the 1950's. Any early (pre-1960) Goebel Disney piece is hard to find and very collectible. The main characters are harder to acquire and rarely seen offered by other dealers.

The Disneykin Playset Store Display shown in Plate 187 was made by Louis Marx and Company. Each of the six playsets are themselves rare but store displays are the pinnacle Disneykin pieces. The number of store displays produced was limited. Another unique store display is the Ludwig Von Drake RCA Store Display in Plate 188. This display advertised the clarity of the picture of "Walt Disney's Wonderful World of Color" because of the use of RCA's Silverama Picture Tubes.

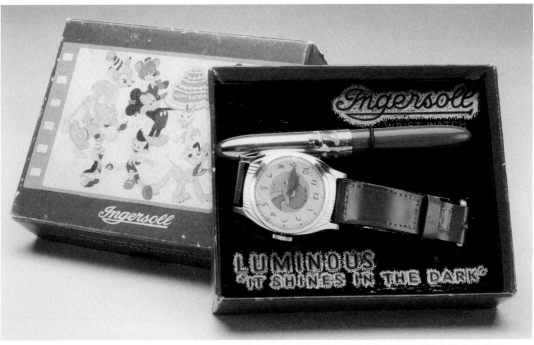

PLATE 178 - BAMBI BIRTHDAY WATCH was made by Ingersoll and is one of a series of six birthday watches. The luminous pen came with the watch. G – $500.00, Ex/M – $550.00.

PLATE 179 - DONALD DUCK DRUMMER *was produced by Linemar and is all in tin. It sold originally for 89¢. G – $950.00, Ex/M – $1,000.00.*

PLATE 180 - *DONALD DUCK DRUMMER. G – $950.00, Ex/M – $1,000.00.*

PLATE 181 - *DONALD DUCK CERAMIC BANK made by the Leeds China Company. G – $60.00, Ex/M – $80.00.*

PLATE 182 - *DONALD DUCK AND NEPHEWS WOOD PULL TOY produced by Fisher-Price. G – $225.00, Ex/M – $250.00.*

PLATE 183 - *SNOW WHITE AND THE SEVEN DWARFS DISNEYKIN SET was made by Marx and the value is much greater in their original boxes. $G – $150.00, Ex/M – $175.00.*

PLATE 184 - *DOPEY CERAMIC PLANTER made by Leeds China Company. G – $50.00, Ex/M – $55.00.*

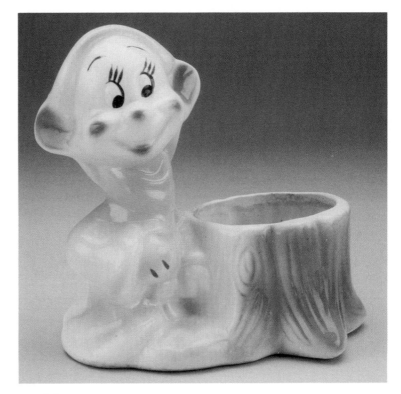

**PLATE 185 - HELBROS BACKWARD GOOFY WATCH** *is one of the most sought-after latter vintage watches. This watch from the 1970's was recently produced as a limited edition watch. G – $1,300.00, Ex/M – $1,500.00.*

**PLATE 186 - SNOW WHITE AND THE SEVEN DWARFS** *are a Goebel product with the stylized Bee marking. Any vintage Goebel Disney figurine is very collectible. G – $450.00, Ex/M – $500.00.*

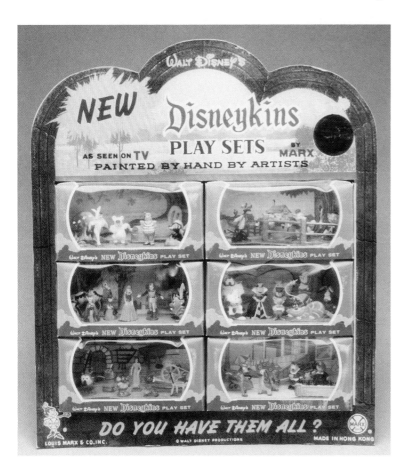

PLATE 187 - *DISNEYKINS PLAY SET STORE DISPLAY was made by Louis Marx & Co. Each of the six play sets themselves are rare but the store display is virtually impossible to find. G – $2,500.00, Ex/M – $3,000.00.*

PLATE 188 - *LUDWIG VON DRAKE RCA STORE DISPLAY was made to advertise RCA's Silverama Picture Tubes. This product was advertised as Walt Disney's "Wonderful World of Color." G – $150.00, Ex/M – $170.00.*

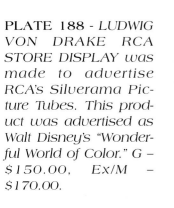

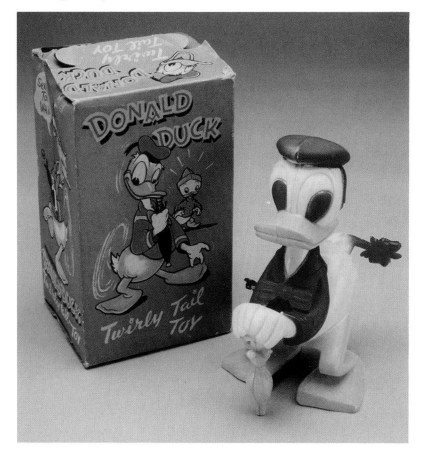

PLATE 189 - *DONALD DUCK TWIRLY TAIL was made by Marx out of plastic. This is a rare version of the box. G – $150.00, Ex/M – $200.00.*

PLATE 190 - *PROFESSOR LUDWIG VON DRAKE TWISTABLE TOY produced by Marx. G – $150.00, Ex/M – $175.00.*

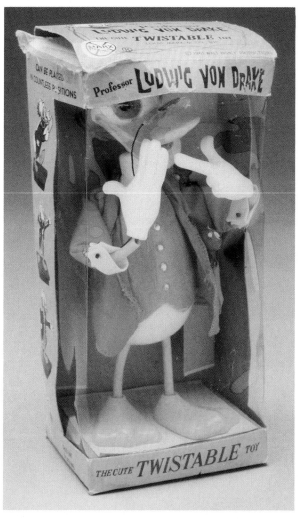

**PLATE 191** - *DISNEY SOAKY TOYS made by Colgate Palmolive held bubble bath.  G – $30.00, Ex/M – $35.00.*

**PLATE 192** - *THREE LITTLE PIGS celluloid was sold at Disneyland in 1959.  G – $100.00, Ex/M – $115.00.*

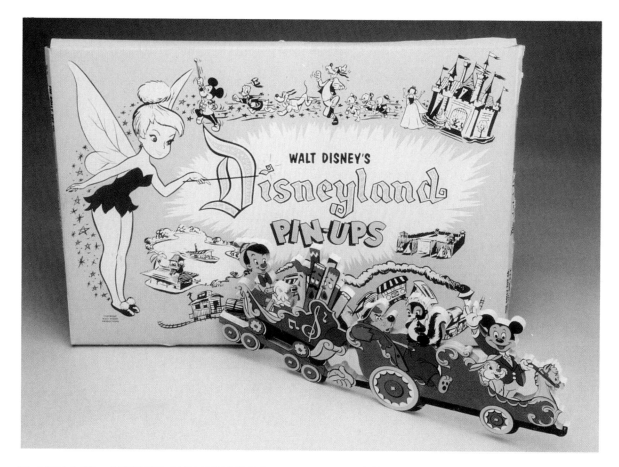

PLATE 193 - *DISNEYLAND PIN-UPS features a train full of Disney characters. G – $75.00, Ex/M – $80.00.*

PLATE 194 - *MICKEY MOUSE CLUB ADVEN-TURE KIT. G – $70.00, Ex/M – $75.00.*

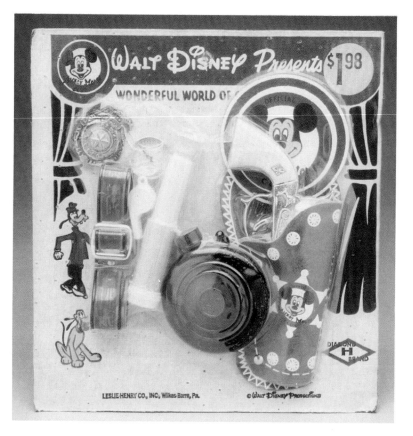

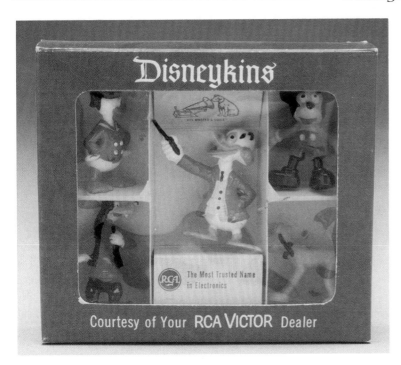

PLATE 195 - *DISNEYKINS DISPLAY given away by RCA Victor dealers. G – $90.00, Ex/M – $110.00.*

PLATE 196 - *TINKER BELLE HAND PUPPET produced by the Gund Company. G – $60.00, Ex/M – $65.00.*

PLATE 197 - *DONALD DUCK BAYARD FRENCH ALARM CLOCK. G – $175.00, Ex/M – $200.00.*

PLATE 198 - *SNOW WHITE (Blanche Neige) BAYARD FRENCH ALARM CLOCK. G – $225.00, Ex/M – $300.00.*

PLATE 199 - *PLUTO BAYARD FRENCH ALARM CLOCK. G – $225.00, Ex/M – $300.00.*

PLATE 200 - *BAMBI BAYARD FRENCH ALARM CLOCK. G – $350.00, Ex/M – $400.00.*

PLATE 201 - *PINOCCHIO BAYARD FRENCH ALARM CLOCK. G – $350.00, Ex/M – $400.00.*

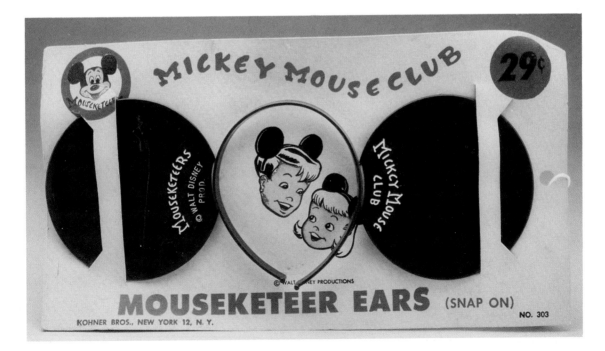

PLATE 202 - *MICKEY MOUSE CLUB MOUSEKETEER EARS made by Kohner Brothers. G – $60.00, Ex/M – $65.00.*

**PLATE 203 - THUMPER CERAMIC PLANTER. G – $35.00, Ex/M – $40.00.**

PLATE 204 - *DISNEY PLASTIC POP-UP CHARACTERS. G – $10.00, Ex/M – $15.00 each.*

**PLATE 205** - *PLUTO WIND UP made by Linemar. The ears are made of a leatherette material. G – $175.00, Ex/M – $200.00.*

**PLATE 206** - *MINNIE MOUSE CERAMIC PLANTER made by Leeds. G – $55.00, Ex/M – $60.00.*

**PLATE 207** - *MICKEY MOUSE ALARM CLOCK was distributed by House Martin. G – $150.00, Ex/M – $175.00.*

PLATE 209 - *DONALD AND DAISY DUCK SALT AND PEPPER SHAKERS are glazed ceramics. G – $25.00, Ex/M – $30.00.*

PLATE 208 - *DONALD DUCK PLASTIC BATH TOY. G – $25.00, Ex/M – $30.00.*

PLATE 210 - *MICKEY MOUSE CAMERA OUTFIT comes with all the necessary equipment. The backside of the box depicts Disneyland. G – $225.00, Ex/M – $250.00.*

PLATE 211 - *MICKEY MOUSE BAYARD FRENCH ALARM CLOCK. G – $175.00, Ex/M – $200.00.*

PLATE 212 - *DISNEYKIN DIS-PLAY shows 34 hand painted Disneykins made by Marx. G – $300.00, Ex/M – $325.00.*

PLATE 213 - *DISNEY CHARACTER HAND PUPPETS. G – $40.00, Ex/M – $45.00 each.*

PLATE 214 - *DOPEY CERAMIC FIG-URINE. G – $35.00, Ex/M – $40.00.*

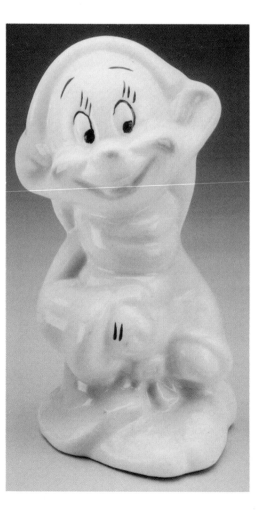

**PLATE 215** - *MICKEY MOUSE WATCH made by Ingersoll. It originally sold for $12.95. G – $325.00, Ex/M – $350.00.*

**PLATE 216 - COCA-COLA 15 YEAR WALT DISNEY WORLD COMMERATIVE SET. G – $50.00, Ex/M – $55.00.**

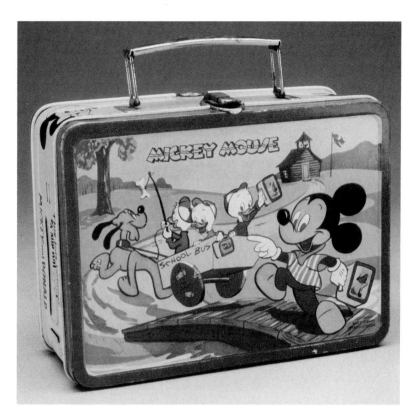

PLATE 217 - *MICKEY MOUSE LUNCH BOX is by ADCO Liberty and is from the 1950's which makes it very desirable. G – $350.00, Ex/M – $400.00.*

PLATE 218 - *ROLYKINS were produced by Marx Toys Co. and were made with a variety of Disney characters. G – $40.00, Ex/M – $45.00.*

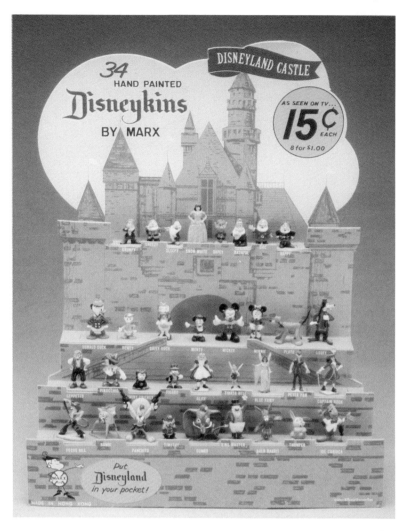

PLATE 219 - *DISNEYKINS DISNEY-LAND CASTLE STORE DISPLAY shows the 34 hand painted Disneykins that were available individually. G – $350.00, Ex/M – $375.00.*

PLATE 220 - *VINTAGE DISNEY REPRODUCTION currently being offered in stores. G – $15.00, Ex/M – $20.00.*

**PLATE 221** - *DONALD DUCK POSTER was designed by Walt Disney for the Food and Nutrition Committee California War Council promoting the value of a good breakfast. G – $275.00, Ex/M – $325.00.*

**PLATE 222** - *DISNEY WORLD TOWN SQUARE sold only at Sears for a very short time. G – $125.00, Ex/M – $130.00.*

PLATE 223 - *MICKEY MOUSE POP-UP COLORFORM SET that utilizes 1930's characters but is a modern toy. G – $15.00, Ex/M – $20.00.*

PLATE 224 - *DISNEYKIN PLAY SETS STORE DISPLAY produced by Marx and displays the 6 Disneykin play sets that were available. G – $3,000.00, Ex/M – $3,500.00*

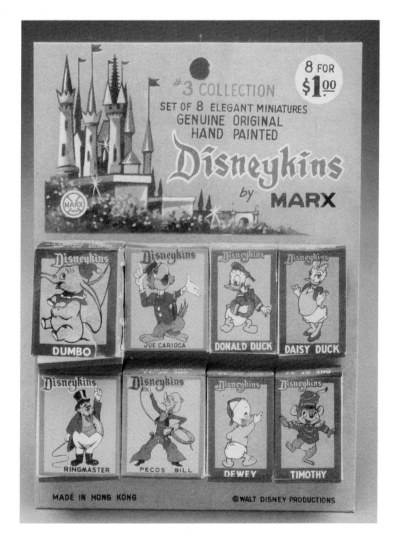

PLATE 226 - SCROOGE MCDUCK WATCH *made by the Lorus Company and sold at major department stores. G – $40.00, Ex/M – $45.00.*

PLATE 225 - *DISNEYKINS COLLECTION BY MARX. G – $200.00, Ex/M – $225.00*

PLATE 227 - DONALD DUCK LORUS QUARTZ WATCH. *G – $40.00, Ex/M – $45.00.*

PLATE 229 - *MINNIE MOUSE PLASTIC RAMP WALKER. G – $20.00, Ex/M – $30.00.*

PLATE 228 - *DONALD DUCK SALT AND PEPPER SHAKERS made of ceramic. G – $60.00, Ex/M – $70.00.*

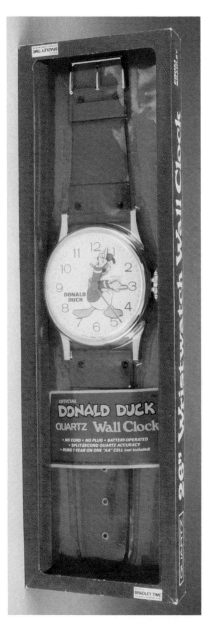

PLATE 230 - *DONALD DUCK QUARTZ WALL CLOCK made by the Bradley Company. G – $70.00, Ex/M – $75.00.*

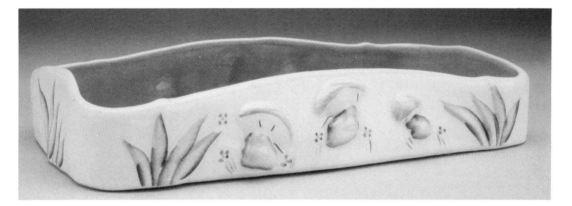

PLATE 231 - *FANTASIA BOWL was produced by Vernon Kilns. G – $300.00, Ex/M – $325.00.*

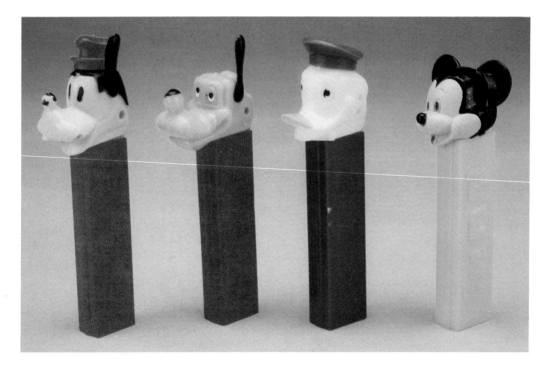

PLATE 232 - *DISNEY PEZ CANDY DISPENSERS. G – $15.00, Ex/M – $20.00.*

PLATE 233 - *WINNIE THE POOH TIE CLASP. G – $10.00, Ex/M – $15.00.*

PLATE 234 - *DOPEY CLOCK is made of wood and the eyes move in time with the pendulum. G – $25.00, Ex/M – $30.00.*

**PLATE 235 - SLEEPING BEAUTY CELLULOID** is an original celluloid from the movie and has multi-images but no background. G – $1,200.00, Ex/M – $1,500.00.

**PLATE 236 - SNAP-EEZE STORE DISPLAY** shows the Marx toys that sold for 39¢ in the 1970's. G – $500.00, Ex/M – $525.00.

PLATE 237 - *SNAP-EEZE STORE DIS-
PLAY listing all the various characters
available. G – $500.00, Ex/M –
$525.00.*

PLATE 238 - *MICKEY'S HAUNTED HOUSE is an electronic action game that used a small metal
ball. G – $250.00, Ex/M – $275.00.*

**PLATE 239** - *PINOCCHIO GLASSES made by the Libby Glass Company. G – $30.00, Ex/M – $35.00 each.*

**PLATE 240** - *MICKEY MOUSE SLUGAROO GAME AND STORE DISPLAY. G – $25.00, Ex/M – $30.00.*

PLATE 241 - *MICKEY MOUSE CLUB DIS-NEYLAND WALLET BY CROYDEN STORE DISPLAY. G – $210.00, Ex/M – $225.00.*

PLATE 242 - *MICKEY MOUSE NOVELTIES SET. G – $25.00, Ex/M – $30.00.*

The author wishes to thank Collector Books for the superb job they do in publishing his price guides. I am always purchasing Disneyana and Beatle collectibles. Please call or write:

Michael Stern
1950 North Park Place
Suite 100
Atlanta, GA 30339
(404) 951-8411

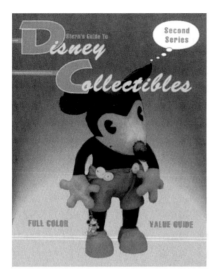

Stern's Guide to DISNEY Collectibles
Second Series
Michael Stern
ISBN: 0-89145-437-3
This second series of Stern's Guide to Disney Collectibles has no repeats of the first edition. Hundreds of examples of Disney collectibles from the golden age to modern. Over 240 photos including virtually every type of Disney collectible.

#2139 • 8½ x 11 • 152 Pgs. • $14.95

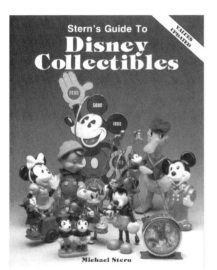

Stern's Guide to DISNEY Collectibles
First Series
Michael Stern
ISBN: 0-89145-369-5
Disney collectors just have to have these popular guides to America's largest comic-character field. This colorful edition is packed full of Disney memorabilia to assist in both dating and pricing various pieces.

#1886 • 8½ x 11 • 128 Pgs. • $14.95

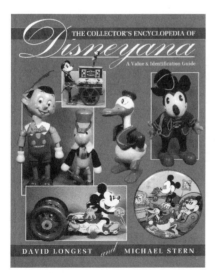

Collector's Encyclopedia of Disneyana
David Longest and Michael Stern
ISBN: 0-89145-500-0
The definitive guide to the golden age of Disneyana. More than 860 full-color photos of common, rare, unusual, and highly collectible Disneyana. Toys are from the 1930's through the early 1960's.

#2338 • 8½ x 11 • 128 Pgs. • $24.95

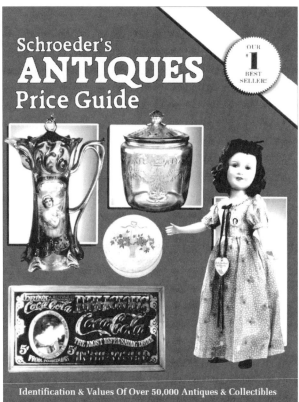